SCRIPTURE JOURNAL

ENGLISH STANDARD VERSION

1–2 CHRONICLES

CROSSWAY

WHEATON, ILLINOIS — ESV.ORG

RRDS		33	32	31	30	29	28	27	26	25	24
15	14	13	12	11	10	9	8	7	6	5	4	3	2	1

PREFACE

The Bible

The words of the Bible are the very words of God our Creator speaking to us. They are completely truthful;[1] they are pure;[2] they are powerful;[3] and they are wise and righteous.[4] We should read these words with reverence and awe,[5] and with joy and delight.[6] Through these words God gives us eternal life,[7] and daily nourishes our spiritual lives.[8]

The ESV Translation

The English Standard Version (ESV) stands in the classic stream of English Bible translations that goes back nearly five centuries. In this stream, accurate faithfulness to the original text is combined with simplicity, beauty, and dignity of expression. Our goal has been to carry forward this legacy for this generation and generations to come.

The ESV is an "essentially literal" translation that seeks as far as possible to reproduce the meaning and structure of the original text and the personal style of each Bible writer. We have sought to be "as literal as possible" while maintaining clear expression and literary excellence. Therefore the ESV is well suited for both personal reading and church ministry, for devotional reflection and serious study, and for Scripture memorization.

---

[1] Ps. 119:160; Prov. 30:5; Titus 1:2; Heb. 6:18 [2] Ps. 12:6 [3] Jer. 23:29; Heb. 4:12; 1 Pet. 1:23 [4] Ps. 19:7–11 [5] Deut. 28:58; Ps. 119:74; Isa. 66:2 [6] Ps. 19:7–11; 119:14, 97, 103; Jer. 15:16 [7] John 6:68; 1 Pet. 1:23 [8] Deut. 32:46; Matt. 4:4

The ESV Publishing Team

The ESV publishing team has included more than a hundred people. The fourteen-member Translation Oversight Committee benefited from the work of fifty biblical experts serving as Translation Review Scholars and from the comments of the more than fifty members of the Advisory Council. This international team from many denominations shares a common commitment to the truth of God's Word and to historic Christian orthodoxy.

To God's Honor and Praise

We know that no Bible translation is perfect; but we also know that God uses imperfect and inadequate things to his honor and praise. So to God the Father, Son, and Holy Spirit—and to his people—we offer what we have done, with our prayers that it may prove useful, with gratitude for much help given, and with ongoing wonder that our God should ever have entrusted to us so momentous a task.

Soli Deo Gloria!—To God alone be the glory!
The Translation Oversight Committee

1 CHRONICLES

From Adam to Abraham

1 Adam, Seth, Enosh; ² Kenan, Mahalalel, Jared; ³ Enoch, Methuselah, Lamech; ⁴ Noah, Shem, Ham, and Japheth.

⁵ The sons of Japheth: Gomer, Magog, Madai, Javan, Tubal, Meshech, and Tiras. ⁶ The sons of Gomer: Ashkenaz, Riphath, and Togarmah. ⁷ The sons of Javan: Elishah, Tarshish, Kittim, and Rodanim.

⁸ The sons of Ham: Cush, Egypt, Put, and Canaan. ⁹ The sons of Cush: Seba, Havilah, Sabta, Raamah, and Sabteca. The sons of Raamah: Sheba and Dedan. ¹⁰ Cush fathered Nimrod. He was the first on earth to be a mighty man.

¹¹ Egypt fathered Ludim, Anamim, Lehabim, Naphtuhim, ¹² Pathrusim, Casluhim (from whom the Philistines came), and Caphtorim.

¹³ Canaan fathered Sidon his firstborn and Heth, ¹⁴ and the Jebusites, the Amorites, the Girgashites, ¹⁵ the Hivites, the Arkites, the Sinites, ¹⁶ the Arvadites, the Zemarites, and the Hamathites.

¹⁷ The sons of Shem: Elam, Asshur, Arpachshad, Lud, and Aram. And the sons of Aram: Uz, Hul, Gether, and Meshech. ¹⁸ Arpachshad fathered Shelah, and Shelah fathered Eber. ¹⁹ To Eber were born two sons: the name of the one was Peleg (for in his days the earth was divided), and his brother's name

was Joktan. [20] Joktan fathered Almodad, Sheleph, Hazarma-veth, Jerah, [21] Hadoram, Uzal, Diklah, [22] Obal, Abimael, Sheba, [23] Ophir, Havilah, and Jobab; all these were the sons of Joktan.

[24] Shem, Arpachshad, Shelah; [25] Eber, Peleg, Reu; [26] Serug, Nahor, Terah; [27] Abram, that is, Abraham.

From Abraham to Jacob

[28] The sons of Abraham: Isaac and Ishmael. [29] These are their genealogies: the firstborn of Ishmael, Nebaioth, and Kedar, Adbeel, Mibsam, [30] Mishma, Dumah, Massa, Hadad, Tema, [31] Jetur, Naphish, and Kedemah. These are the sons of Ishmael. [32] The sons of Keturah, Abraham's concubine: she bore Zimran, Jokshan, Medan, Midian, Ishbak, and Shuah. The sons of Jokshan: Sheba and Dedan. [33] The sons of Midian: Ephah, Epher, Hanoch, Abida, and Eldaah. All these were the descendants of Keturah.

[34] Abraham fathered Isaac. The sons of Isaac: Esau and Israel. [35] The sons of Esau: Eliphaz, Reuel, Jeush, Jalam, and Korah. [36] The sons of Eliphaz: Teman, Omar, Zepho, Gatam, Kenaz, and of Timna, Amalek. [37] The sons of Reuel: Nahath, Zerah, Shammah, and Mizzah.

[38] The sons of Seir: Lotan, Shobal, Zibeon, Anah, Dishon, Ezer, and Dishan. [39] The sons of Lotan: Hori and Hemam; and Lotan's sister was Timna. [40] The sons of Shobal: Alvan, Manahath, Ebal, Shepho, and Onam. The sons of Zibeon: Aiah and Anah. [41] The son of Anah: Dishon. The sons of Dishon: Hemdan, Eshban, Ithran, and Cheran. [42] The sons of Ezer: Bilhan, Zaavan, and Akan. The sons of Dishan: Uz and Aran.

[43] These are the kings who reigned in the land of Edom before any king reigned over the people of Israel: Bela the son

of Beor, the name of his city being Dinhabah. ⁴⁴ Bela died, and Jobab the son of Zerah of Bozrah reigned in his place. ⁴⁵ Jobab died, and Husham of the land of the Temanites reigned in his place. ⁴⁶ Husham died, and Hadad the son of Bedad, who defeated Midian in the country of Moab, reigned in his place, the name of his city being Avith. ⁴⁷ Hadad died, and Samlah of Masrekah reigned in his place. ⁴⁸ Samlah died, and Shaul of Rehoboth on the Euphrates reigned in his place. ⁴⁹ Shaul died, and Baal-hanan, the son of Achbor, reigned in his place. ⁵⁰ Baal-hanan died, and Hadad reigned in his place, the name of his city being Pai; and his wife's name was Mehetabel, the daughter of Matred, the daughter of Mezahab. ⁵¹ And Hadad died.

The chiefs of Edom were: chiefs Timna, Alvah, Jetheth, ⁵² Oholibamah, Elah, Pinon, ⁵³ Kenaz, Teman, Mibzar, ⁵⁴ Magdiel, and Iram; these are the chiefs of Edom.

A Genealogy of David

2 These are the sons of Israel: Reuben, Simeon, Levi, Judah, Issachar, Zebulun, ² Dan, Joseph, Benjamin, Naphtali, Gad, and Asher. ³ The sons of Judah: Er, Onan and Shelah; these three Bath-shua the Canaanite bore to him. Now Er, Judah's firstborn, was evil in the sight of the LORD, and he put him to death. ⁴ His daughter-in-law Tamar also bore him Perez and Zerah. Judah had five sons in all.

⁵ The sons of Perez: Hezron and Hamul. ⁶ The sons of Zerah: Zimri, Ethan, Heman, Calcol, and Dara, five in all. ⁷ The son of Carmi: Achan, the troubler of Israel, who broke faith in the matter of the devoted thing; ⁸ and Ethan's son was Azariah.

⁹ The sons of Hezron that were born to him: Jerahmeel, Ram, and Chelubai. ¹⁰ Ram fathered Amminadab, and Amminadab

fathered Nahshon, prince of the sons of Judah. ¹¹ Nahshon fathered Salmon, Salmon fathered Boaz, ¹² Boaz fathered Obed, Obed fathered Jesse. ¹³ Jesse fathered Eliab his firstborn, Abinadab the second, Shimea the third, ¹⁴ Nethanel the fourth, Raddai the fifth, ¹⁵ Ozem the sixth, David the seventh. ¹⁶ And their sisters were Zeruiah and Abigail. The sons of Zeruiah: Abishai, Joab, and Asahel, three. ¹⁷ Abigail bore Amasa, and the father of Amasa was Jether the Ishmaelite.

¹⁸ Caleb the son of Hezron fathered children by his wife Azubah, and by Jerioth; and these were her sons: Jesher, Shobab, and Ardon. ¹⁹ When Azubah died, Caleb married Ephrath, who bore him Hur. ²⁰ Hur fathered Uri, and Uri fathered Bezalel.

²¹ Afterward Hezron went in to the daughter of Machir the father of Gilead, whom he married when he was sixty years old, and she bore him Segub. ²² And Segub fathered Jair, who had twenty-three cities in the land of Gilead. ²³ But Geshur and Aram took from them Havvoth-jair, Kenath, and its villages, sixty towns. All these were descendants of Machir, the father of Gilead. ²⁴ After the death of Hezron, Caleb went in to Ephrathah, the wife of Hezron his father, and she bore him Ashhur, the father of Tekoa.

²⁵ The sons of Jerahmeel, the firstborn of Hezron: Ram, his firstborn, Bunah, Oren, Ozem, and Ahijah. ²⁶ Jerahmeel also had another wife, whose name was Atarah; she was the mother of Onam. ²⁷ The sons of Ram, the firstborn of Jerahmeel: Maaz, Jamin, and Eker. ²⁸ The sons of Onam: Shammai and Jada. The sons of Shammai: Nadab and Abishur. ²⁹ The name of Abishur's wife was Abihail, and she bore him Ahban and Molid. ³⁰ The sons of Nadab: Seled and Appaim; and Seled died childless. ³¹ The son of Appaim: Ishi. The son of Ishi: Sheshan. The son of

Sheshan: Ahlai. ³² The sons of Jada, Shammai's brother: Jether and Jonathan; and Jether died childless. ³³ The sons of Jonathan: Peleth and Zaza. These were the descendants of Jerahmeel. ³⁴ Now Sheshan had no sons, only daughters, but Sheshan had an Egyptian slave whose name was Jarha. ³⁵ So Sheshan gave his daughter in marriage to Jarha his slave, and she bore him Attai. ³⁶ Attai fathered Nathan, and Nathan fathered Zabad. ³⁷ Zabad fathered Ephlal, and Ephlal fathered Obed. ³⁸ Obed fathered Jehu, and Jehu fathered Azariah. ³⁹ Azariah fathered Helez, and Helez fathered Eleasah. ⁴⁰ Eleasah fathered Sismai, and Sismai fathered Shallum. ⁴¹ Shallum fathered Jekamiah, and Jekamiah fathered Elishama.

⁴² The sons of Caleb the brother of Jerahmeel: Mareshah his firstborn, who fathered Ziph. The son of Mareshah: Hebron. ⁴³ The sons of Hebron: Korah, Tappuah, Rekem and Shema. ⁴⁴ Shema fathered Raham, the father of Jorkeam; and Rekem fathered Shammai. ⁴⁵ The son of Shammai: Maon; and Maon fathered Beth-zur. ⁴⁶ Ephah also, Caleb's concubine, bore Haran, Moza, and Gazez; and Haran fathered Gazez. ⁴⁷ The sons of Jahdai: Regem, Jotham, Geshan, Pelet, Ephah, and Shaaph. ⁴⁸ Maacah, Caleb's concubine, bore Sheber and Tirhanah. ⁴⁹ She also bore Shaaph the father of Madmannah, Sheva the father of Machbenah and the father of Gibea; and the daughter of Caleb was Achsah. ⁵⁰ These were the descendants of Caleb.

The sons of Hur the firstborn of Ephrathah: Shobal the father of Kiriath-jearim, ⁵¹ Salma, the father of Bethlehem, and Hareph the father of Beth-gader. ⁵² Shobal the father of Kiriath-jearim had other sons: Haroeh, half of the Menuhoth. ⁵³ And the clans of Kiriath-jearim: the Ithrites, the Puthites, the Shumathites, and the Mishraites; from these came the

Zorathites and the Eshtaolites. ⁵⁴ The sons of Salma: Bethlehem, the Netophathites, Atroth-beth-joab and half of the Mana-hathites, the Zorites. ⁵⁵ The clans also of the scribes who lived at Jabez: the Tirathites, the Shimeathites and the Sucathites. These are the Kenites who came from Hammath, the father of the house of Rechab.

Descendants of David

3 These are the sons of David who were born to him in Hebron: the firstborn, Amnon, by Ahinoam the Jezreelite; the second, Daniel, by Abigail the Carmelite, ² the third, Absalom, whose mother was Maacah, the daughter of Talmai, king of Geshur; the fourth, Adonijah, whose mother was Haggith; ³ the fifth, Shephatiah, by Abital; the sixth, Ithream, by his wife Eglah; ⁴ six were born to him in Hebron, where he reigned for seven years and six months. And he reigned thirty-three years in Jerusalem. ⁵ These were born to him in Jerusalem: Shimea, Shobab, Nathan and Solomon, four by Bath-shua, the daughter of Ammiel; ⁶ then Ibhar, Elishama, Eliphelet, ⁷ Nogah, Nepheg, Japhia, ⁸ Elishama, Eliada, and Eliphelet, nine. ⁹ All these were David's sons, besides the sons of the concubines, and Tamar was their sister.

¹⁰ The son of Solomon was Rehoboam, Abijah his son, Asa his son, Jehoshaphat his son, ¹¹ Joram his son, Ahaziah his son, Joash his son, ¹² Amaziah his son, Azariah his son, Jotham his son, ¹³ Ahaz his son, Hezekiah his son, Manasseh his son, ¹⁴ Amon his son, Josiah his son. ¹⁵ The sons of Josiah: Johanan the firstborn, the second Jehoiakim, the third Zedekiah, the fourth Shallum. ¹⁶ The descendants of Jehoiakim: Jeconiah his son, Zedekiah his son; ¹⁷ and the sons of Jeconiah, the captive: Shealtiel his son,

¹⁸ Malchiram, Pedaiah, Shenazzar, Jekamiah, Hoshama and Nedabiah; ¹⁹ and the sons of Pedaiah: Zerubbabel and Shimei; and the sons of Zerubbabel: Meshullam and Hananiah, and Shelomith was their sister; ²⁰ and Hashubah, Ohel, Berechiah, Hasadiah, and Jushab-hesed, five. ²¹ The sons of Hananiah: Pelatiah and Jeshaiah, his son Rephaiah, his son Arnan, his son Obadiah, his son Shecaniah. ²² The son of Shecaniah: Shemaiah. And the sons of Shemaiah: Hattush, Igal, Bariah, Neariah, and Shaphat, six. ²³ The sons of Neariah: Elioenai, Hizkiah, and Azrikam, three. ²⁴ The sons of Elioenai: Hodaviah, Eliashib, Pelaiah, Akkub, Johanan, Delaiah, and Anani, seven.

Descendants of Judah

4 The sons of Judah: Perez, Hezron, Carmi, Hur, and Shobal. ² Reaiah the son of Shobal fathered Jahath, and Jahath fathered Ahumai and Lahad. These were the clans of the Zorathites. ³ These were the sons of Etam: Jezreel, Ishma, and Idbash; and the name of their sister was Hazzelelponi, ⁴ and Penuel fathered Gedor, and Ezer fathered Hushah. These were the sons of Hur, the firstborn of Ephrathah, the father of Bethlehem. ⁵ Ashhur, the father of Tekoa, had two wives, Helah and Naarah; ⁶ Naarah bore him Ahuzzam, Hepher, Temeni, and Haahashtari. These were the sons of Naarah. ⁷ The sons of Helah: Zereth, Izhar, and Ethnan. ⁸ Koz fathered Anub, Zobebah, and the clans of Aharhel, the son of Harum. ⁹ Jabez was more honorable than his brothers; and his mother called his name Jabez, saying, "Because I bore him in pain." ¹⁰ Jabez called upon the God of Israel, saying, "Oh that you would bless me and enlarge my border, and that your hand might be with me, and that you would keep me from harm so that it might

not bring me pain!" And God granted what he asked. ¹¹ Chelub, the brother of Shuhah, fathered Mehir, who fathered Eshton. ¹² Eshton fathered Beth-rapha, Paseah, and Tehinnah, the father of Ir-nahash. These are the men of Recah. ¹³ The sons of Kenaz: Othniel and Seraiah; and the sons of Othniel: Hathath and Meonothai. ¹⁴ Meonothai fathered Ophrah; and Seraiah fathered Joab, the father of Ge-harashim, so-called because they were craftsmen. ¹⁵ The sons of Caleb the son of Jephunneh: Iru, Elah, and Naam; and the son of Elah: Kenaz. ¹⁶ The sons of Jehallelel: Ziph, Ziphah, Tiria, and Asarel. ¹⁷ The sons of Ezrah: Jether, Mered, Epher, and Jalon. These are the sons of Bithiah, the daughter of Pharaoh, whom Mered married; and she conceived and bore Miriam, Shammai, and Ishbah, the father of Eshtemoa. ¹⁸ And his Judahite wife bore Jered the father of Gedor, Heber the father of Soco, and Jekuthiel the father of Zanoah. ¹⁹ The sons of the wife of Hodiah, the sister of Naham, were the fathers of Keilah the Garmite and Eshtemoa the Maacathite. ²⁰ The sons of Shimon: Amnon, Rinnah, Ben-hanan, and Tilon. The sons of Ishi: Zoheth and Ben-zoheth. ²¹ The sons of Shelah the son of Judah: Er the father of Lecah, Laadah the father of Mareshah, and the clans of the house of linen workers at Beth-ashbea; ²² and Jokim, and the men of Cozeba, and Joash, and Saraph, who ruled in Moab and returned to Lehem (now the records are ancient). ²³ These were the potters who were inhabitants of Netaim and Gederah. They lived there in the king's service.

Descendants of Simeon

²⁴ The sons of Simeon: Nemuel, Jamin, Jarib, Zerah, Shaul; ²⁵ Shallum was his son, Mibsam his son, Mishma his son.

²⁶ The sons of Mishma: Hammuel his son, Zaccur his son, Shimei his son. ²⁷ Shimei had sixteen sons and six daughters; but his brothers did not have many children, nor did all their clan multiply like the men of Judah. ²⁸ They lived in Beersheba, Moladah, Hazar-shual, ²⁹ Bilhah, Ezem, Tolad, ³⁰ Bethuel, Hormah, Ziklag, ³¹ Beth-marcaboth, Hazar-susim, Beth-biri, and Shaaraim. These were their cities until David reigned. ³² And their villages were Etam, Ain, Rimmon, Tochen, and Ashan, five cities, ³³ along with all their villages that were around these cities as far as Baal. These were their settlements, and they kept a genealogical record.

³⁴ Meshobab, Jamlech, Joshah the son of Amaziah, ³⁵ Joel, Jehu the son of Joshibiah, son of Seraiah, son of Asiel, ³⁶ Elioenai, Jaakobah, Jeshohaiah, Asaiah, Adiel, Jesimiel, Benaiah, ³⁷ Ziza the son of Shiphi, son of Allon, son of Jedaiah, son of Shimri, son of Shemaiah— ³⁸ these mentioned by name were princes in their clans, and their fathers' houses increased greatly. ³⁹ They journeyed to the entrance of Gedor, to the east side of the valley, to seek pasture for their flocks, ⁴⁰ where they found rich, good pasture, and the land was very broad, quiet, and peaceful, for the former inhabitants there belonged to Ham. ⁴¹ These, registered by name, came in the days of Hezekiah, king of Judah, and destroyed their tents and the Meunites who were found there, and marked them for destruction to this day, and settled in their place, because there was pasture there for their flocks. ⁴² And some of them, five hundred men of the Simeonites, went to Mount Seir, having as their leaders Pelatiah, Neariah, Rephaiah, and Uzziel, the sons of Ishi. ⁴³ And they defeated the remnant of the Amalekites who had escaped, and they have lived there to this day.

Descendants of Reuben

5 The sons of Reuben the firstborn of Israel (for he was the firstborn, but because he defiled his father's couch, his birthright was given to the sons of Joseph the son of Israel, so that he could not be enrolled as the oldest son; ² though Judah became strong among his brothers and a chief came from him, yet the birthright belonged to Joseph), ³ the sons of Reuben, the firstborn of Israel: Hanoch, Pallu, Hezron, and Carmi. ⁴ The sons of Joel: Shemaiah his son, Gog his son, Shimei his son, ⁵ Micah his son, Reaiah his son, Baal his son, ⁶ Beerah his son, whom Tiglath-pileser king of Assyria carried away into exile; he was a chief of the Reubenites. ⁷ And his kinsmen by their clans, when the genealogy of their generations was recorded: the chief, Jeiel, and Zechariah, ⁸ and Bela the son of Azaz, son of Shema, son of Joel, who lived in Aroer, as far as Nebo and Baal-meon. ⁹ He also lived to the east as far as the entrance of the desert this side of the Euphrates, because their livestock had multiplied in the land of Gilead. ¹⁰ And in the days of Saul they waged war against the Hagrites, who fell into their hand. And they lived in their tents throughout all the region east of Gilead.

Descendants of Gad

¹¹ The sons of Gad lived over against them in the land of Bashan as far as Salecah: ¹² Joel the chief, Shapham the second, Janai, and Shaphat in Bashan. ¹³ And their kinsmen according to their fathers' houses: Michael, Meshullam, Sheba, Jorai, Jacan, Zia and Eber, seven. ¹⁴ These were the sons of Abihail the son of Huri, son of Jaroah, son of Gilead, son of Michael, son of Jeshishai, son of Jahdo, son of Buz. ¹⁵ Ahi the son of Abdiel, son of Guni, was chief in their fathers' houses, ¹⁶ and they lived in

Gilead, in Bashan and in its towns, and in all the pasturelands of Sharon to their limits. ¹⁷ All of these were recorded in genealogies in the days of Jotham king of Judah, and in the days of Jeroboam king of Israel.

¹⁸ The Reubenites, the Gadites, and the half-tribe of Manasseh had valiant men who carried shield and sword, and drew the bow, expert in war, 44,760, able to go to war. ¹⁹ They waged war against the Hagrites, Jetur, Naphish, and Nodab. ²⁰ And when they prevailed over them, the Hagrites and all who were with them were given into their hands, for they cried out to God in the battle, and he granted their urgent plea because they trusted in him. ²¹ They carried off their livestock: 50,000 of their camels, 250,000 sheep, 2,000 donkeys, and 100,000 men alive. ²² For many fell, because the war was of God. And they lived in their place until the exile.

The Half-Tribe of Manasseh

²³ The members of the half-tribe of Manasseh lived in the land. They were very numerous from Bashan to Baal-hermon, Senir, and Mount Hermon. ²⁴ These were the heads of their fathers' houses: Epher, Ishi, Eliel, Azriel, Jeremiah, Hodaviah, and Jahdiel, mighty warriors, famous men, heads of their fathers' houses. ²⁵ But they broke faith with the God of their fathers, and whored after the gods of the peoples of the land, whom God had destroyed before them. ²⁶ So the God of Israel stirred up the spirit of Pul king of Assyria, the spirit of Tiglath-pileser king of Assyria, and he took them into exile, namely, the Reubenites, the Gadites, and the half-tribe of Manasseh, and brought them to Halah, Habor, Hara, and the river Gozan, to this day.

Descendants of Levi

6 The sons of Levi: Gershon, Kohath, and Merari. ²The sons of Kohath: Amram, Izhar, Hebron, and Uzziel. ³The children of Amram: Aaron, Moses, and Miriam. The sons of Aaron: Nadab, Abihu, Eleazar, and Ithamar. ⁴Eleazar fathered Phinehas, Phinehas fathered Abishua, ⁵Abishua fathered Bukki, Bukki fathered Uzzi, ⁶Uzzi fathered Zerahiah, Zerahiah fathered Meraioth, ⁷Meraioth fathered Amariah, Amariah fathered Ahitub, ⁸Ahitub fathered Zadok, Zadok fathered Ahimaaz, ⁹Ahimaaz fathered Azariah, Azariah fathered Johanan, ¹⁰and Johanan fathered Azariah (it was he who served as priest in the house that Solomon built in Jerusalem). ¹¹Azariah fathered Amariah, Amariah fathered Ahitub, ¹²Ahitub fathered Zadok, Zadok fathered Shallum, ¹³Shallum fathered Hilkiah, Hilkiah fathered Azariah, ¹⁴Azariah fathered Seraiah, Seraiah fathered Jehozadak; ¹⁵and Jehozadak went into exile when the LORD sent Judah and Jerusalem into exile by the hand of Nebuchadnezzar.

¹⁶The sons of Levi: Gershom, Kohath, and Merari. ¹⁷And these are the names of the sons of Gershom: Libni and Shimei. ¹⁸The sons of Kohath: Amram, Izhar, Hebron and Uzziel. ¹⁹The sons of Merari: Mahli and Mushi. These are the clans of the Levites according to their fathers. ²⁰Of Gershom: Libni his son, Jahath his son, Zimmah his son, ²¹Joah his son, Iddo his son, Zerah his son, Jeatherai his son. ²²The sons of Kohath: Amminadab his son, Korah his son, Assir his son, ²³Elkanah his son, Ebiasaph his son, Assir his son, ²⁴Tahath his son, Uriel his son, Uzziah his son, and Shaul his son. ²⁵The sons of Elkanah: Amasai and Ahimoth, ²⁶Elkanah his son, Zophai his son, Nahath his son, ²⁷Eliab his son, Jeroham his son, Elkanah his son. ²⁸The sons of Samuel: Joel his firstborn, the second Abijah. ²⁹The sons of

Merari: Mahli, Libni his son, Shimei his son, Uzzah his son, ³⁰ Shimea his son, Haggiah his son, and Asaiah his son.

³¹ These are the men whom David put in charge of the service of song in the house of the LORD after the ark rested there. ³² They ministered with song before the tabernacle of the tent of meeting until Solomon built the house of the LORD in Jerusalem, and they performed their service according to their order. ³³ These are the men who served and their sons. Of the sons of the Kohathites: Heman the singer the son of Joel, son of Samuel, ³⁴ son of Elkanah, son of Jeroham, son of Eliel, son of Toah, ³⁵ son of Zuph, son of Elkanah, son of Mahath, son of Amasai, ³⁶ son of Elkanah, son of Joel, son of Azariah, son of Zephaniah, ³⁷ son of Tahath, son of Assir, son of Ebiasaph, son of Korah, ³⁸ son of Izhar, son of Kohath, son of Levi, son of Israel; ³⁹ and his brother Asaph, who stood on his right hand, namely, Asaph the son of Berechiah, son of Shimea, ⁴⁰ son of Michael, son of Baaseiah, son of Malchijah, ⁴¹ son of Ethni, son of Zerah, son of Adaiah, ⁴² son of Ethan, son of Zimmah, son of Shimei, ⁴³ son of Jahath, son of Gershom, son of Levi. ⁴⁴ On the left hand were their brothers, the sons of Merari: Ethan the son of Kishi, son of Abdi, son of Malluch, ⁴⁵ son of Hashabiah, son of Amaziah, son of Hilkiah, ⁴⁶ son of Amzi, son of Bani, son of Shemer, ⁴⁷ son of Mahli, son of Mushi, son of Merari, son of Levi. ⁴⁸ And their brothers the Levites were appointed for all the service of the tabernacle of the house of God.

⁴⁹ But Aaron and his sons made offerings on the altar of burnt offering and on the altar of incense for all the work of the Most Holy Place, and to make atonement for Israel, according to all that Moses the servant of God had commanded. ⁵⁰ These are the sons of Aaron: Eleazar his son, Phinehas his son,

Abishua his son, ⁵¹ Bukki his son, Uzzi his son, Zerahiah his son, ⁵² Meraioth his son, Amariah his son, Ahitub his son, ⁵³ Zadok his son, Ahimaaz his son.

⁵⁴ These are their dwelling places according to their settlements within their borders: to the sons of Aaron of the clans of Kohathites, for theirs was the first lot, ⁵⁵ to them they gave Hebron in the land of Judah and its surrounding pasturelands, ⁵⁶ but the fields of the city and its villages they gave to Caleb the son of Jephunneh. ⁵⁷ To the sons of Aaron they gave the cities of refuge: Hebron, Libnah with its pasturelands, Jattir, Eshtemoa with its pasturelands, ⁵⁸ Hilen with its pasturelands, Debir with its pasturelands, ⁵⁹ Ashan with its pasturelands, and Beth-shemesh with its pasturelands; ⁶⁰ and from the tribe of Benjamin, Gibeon, Geba with its pasturelands, Alemeth with its pasturelands, and Anathoth with its pasturelands. All their cities throughout their clans were thirteen.

⁶¹ To the rest of the Kohathites were given by lot out of the clan of the tribe, out of the half-tribe, the half of Manasseh, ten cities. ⁶² To the Gershomites according to their clans were allotted thirteen cities out of the tribes of Issachar, Asher, Naphtali and Manasseh in Bashan. ⁶³ To the Merarites according to their clans were allotted twelve cities out of the tribes of Reuben, Gad, and Zebulun. ⁶⁴ So the people of Israel gave the Levites the cities with their pasturelands. ⁶⁵ They gave by lot out of the tribes of Judah, Simeon, and Benjamin these cities that are mentioned by name.

⁶⁶ And some of the clans of the sons of Kohath had cities of their territory out of the tribe of Ephraim. ⁶⁷ They were given the cities of refuge: Shechem with its pasturelands in the hill country of Ephraim, Gezer with its pasturelands, ⁶⁸ Jokmeam

with its pasturelands, Beth-horon with its pasturelands, ⁶⁹ Aijalon with its pasturelands, Gath-rimmon with its pasture-lands, ⁷⁰ and out of the half-tribe of Manasseh, Aner with its pasturelands, and Bileam with its pasturelands, for the rest of the clans of the Kohathites.

⁷¹ To the Gershomites were given out of the clan of the half-tribe of Manasseh: Golan in Bashan with its pasturelands and Ashtaroth with its pasturelands; ⁷² and out of the tribe of Issachar: Kedesh with its pasturelands, Daberath with its pas-turelands, ⁷³ Ramoth with its pasturelands, and Anem with its pasturelands; ⁷⁴ out of the tribe of Asher: Mashal with its pasturelands, Abdon with its pasturelands, ⁷⁵ Hukok with its pasturelands, and Rehob with its pasturelands; ⁷⁶ and out of the tribe of Naphtali: Kedesh in Galilee with its pasturelands, Hammon with its pasturelands, and Kiriathaim with its pas-turelands. ⁷⁷ To the rest of the Merarites were allotted out of the tribe of Zebulun: Rimmono with its pasturelands, Tabor with its pasturelands, ⁷⁸ and beyond the Jordan at Jericho, on the east side of the Jordan, out of the tribe of Reuben: Bezer in the wilderness with its pasturelands, Jahzah with its pasturelands, ⁷⁹ Kedemoth with its pasturelands, and Mephaath with its pas-turelands; ⁸⁰ and out of the tribe of Gad: Ramoth in Gilead with its pasturelands, Mahanaim with its pasturelands, ⁸¹ Heshbon with its pasturelands, and Jazer with its pasturelands.

Descendants of Issachar

7 The sons of Issachar: Tola, Puah, Jashub, and Shimron, four. ² The sons of Tola: Uzzi, Rephaiah, Jeriel, Jahmai, Ibsam, and Shemuel, heads of their fathers' houses, namely of Tola, mighty warriors of their generations, their number in

the days of David being 22,600. ³ The son of Uzzi: Izrahiah. And the sons of Izrahiah: Michael, Obadiah, Joel, and Isshiah, all five of them were chief men. ⁴ And along with them, by their generations, according to their fathers' houses, were units of the army for war, 36,000, for they had many wives and sons. ⁵ Their kinsmen belonging to all the clans of Issachar were in all 87,000 mighty warriors, enrolled by genealogy.

Descendants of Benjamin

⁶ The sons of Benjamin: Bela, Becher, and Jediael, three. ⁷ The sons of Bela: Ezbon, Uzzi, Uzziel, Jerimoth, and Iri, five, heads of fathers' houses, mighty warriors. And their enrollment by genealogies was 22,034. ⁸ The sons of Becher: Zemirah, Joash, Eliezer, Elioenai, Omri, Jeremoth, Abijah, Anathoth, and Alemeth. All these were the sons of Becher. ⁹ And their enrollment by genealogies, according to their generations, as heads of their fathers' houses, mighty warriors, was 20,200. ¹⁰ The son of Jediael: Bilhan. And the sons of Bilhan: Jeush, Benjamin, Ehud, Chenaanah, Zethan, Tarshish, and Ahishahar. ¹¹ All these were the sons of Jediael according to the heads of their fathers' houses, mighty warriors, 17,200, able to go to war. ¹² And Shuppim and Huppim were the sons of Ir, Hushim the son of Aher.

Descendants of Naphtali

¹³ The sons of Naphtali: Jahziel, Guni, Jezer and Shallum, the descendants of Bilhah.

Descendants of Manasseh

¹⁴ The sons of Manasseh: Asriel, whom his Aramean concubine bore; she bore Machir the father of Gilead. ¹⁵ And Machir

took a wife for Huppim and for Shuppim. The name of his sister was Maacah. And the name of the second was Zelophehad, and Zelophehad had daughters. ¹⁶ And Maacah the wife of Machir bore a son, and she called his name Peresh; and the name of his brother was Sheresh; and his sons were Ulam and Rakem. ¹⁷ The son of Ulam: Bedan. These were the sons of Gilead the son of Machir, son of Manasseh. ¹⁸ And his sister Hammolecheth bore Ishhod, Abiezer, and Mahlah. ¹⁹ The sons of Shemida were Ahian, Shechem, Likhi, and Aniam.

Descendants of Ephraim

²⁰ The sons of Ephraim: Shuthelah, and Bered his son, Tahath his son, Eleadah his son, Tahath his son, ²¹ Zabad his son, Shuthelah his son, and Ezer and Elead, whom the men of Gath who were born in the land killed, because they came down to raid their livestock. ²² And Ephraim their father mourned many days, and his brothers came to comfort him. ²³ And Ephraim went in to his wife, and she conceived and bore a son. And he called his name Beriah, because disaster had befallen his house. ²⁴ His daughter was Sheerah, who built both Lower and Upper Beth-horon, and Uzzen-sheerah. ²⁵ Rephah was his son, Resheph his son, Telah his son, Tahan his son, ²⁶ Ladan his son, Ammihud his son, Elishama his son, ²⁷ Nun his son, Joshua his son. ²⁸ Their possessions and settlements were Bethel and its towns, and to the east Naaran, and to the west Gezer and its towns, Shechem and its towns, and Ayyah and its towns; ²⁹ also in possession of the Manassites, Beth-shean and its towns, Taanach and its towns, Megiddo and its towns, Dor and its towns. In these lived the sons of Joseph the son of Israel.

Descendants of Asher

[30] The sons of Asher: Imnah, Ishvah, Ishvi, Beriah, and their sister Serah. [31] The sons of Beriah: Heber, and Malchiel, who fathered Birzaith. [32] Heber fathered Japhlet, Shomer, Hotham, and their sister Shua. [33] The sons of Japhlet: Pasach, Bimhal, and Ashvath. These are the sons of Japhlet. [34] The sons of Shemer his brother: Rohgah, Jehubbah, and Aram. [35] The sons of Helem his brother: Zophah, Imna, Shelesh, and Amal. [36] The sons of Zophah: Suah, Harnepher, Shual, Beri, Imrah. [37] Bezer, Hod, Shamma, Shilshah, Ithran, and Beera. [38] The sons of Jether: Jephunneh, Pispa, and Ara. [39] The sons of Ulla: Arah, Hanniel, and Rizia. [40] All of these were men of Asher, heads of fathers' houses, approved, mighty warriors, chiefs of the princes. Their number enrolled by genealogies, for service in war, was 26,000 men.

A Genealogy of Saul

8 Benjamin fathered Bela his firstborn, Ashbel the second, Aharah the third, [2] Nohah the fourth, and Rapha the fifth. [3] And Bela had sons: Addar, Gera, Abihud, [4] Abishua, Naaman, Ahoah, [5] Gera, Shephuphan, and Huram. [6] These are the sons of Ehud (they were heads of fathers' houses of the inhabitants of Geba, and they were carried into exile to Manahath): [7] Naaman, Ahijah, and Gera, that is, Heglam, who fathered Uzza and Ahihud. [8] And Shaharaim fathered sons in the country of Moab after he had sent away Hushim and Baara his wives. [9] He fathered sons by Hodesh his wife: Jobab, Zibia, Mesha, Malcam, [10] Jeuz, Sachia, and Mirmah. These were his sons, heads of fathers' houses. [11] He also fathered sons by Hushim: Abitub and Elpaal. [12] The sons of Elpaal: Eber, Misham, and

Shemed, who built Ono and Lod with its towns, [13] and Beriah and Shema (they were heads of fathers' houses of the inhabitants of Aijalon, who caused the inhabitants of Gath to flee); [14] and Ahio, Shashak, and Jeremoth. [15] Zebadiah, Arad, Eder, [16] Michael, Ishpah, and Joha were sons of Beriah. [17] Zebadiah, Meshullam, Hizki, Heber, [18] Ishmerai, Izliah, and Jobab were the sons of Elpaal. [19] Jakim, Zichri, Zabdi, [20] Elienai, Zillethai, Eliel, [21] Adaiah, Beraiah, and Shimrath were the sons of Shimei. [22] Ishpan, Eber, Eliel, [23] Abdon, Zichri, Hanan, [24] Hananiah, Elam, Anthothijah, [25] Iphdeiah, and Penuel were the sons of Shashak. [26] Shamsherai, Shehariah, Athaliah, [27] Jaareshiah, Elijah, and Zichri were the sons of Jeroham. [28] These were the heads of fathers' houses, according to their generations, chief men. These lived in Jerusalem.

[29] Jeiel the father of Gibeon lived in Gibeon, and the name of his wife was Maacah. [30] His firstborn son: Abdon, then Zur, Kish, Baal, Nadab, [31] Gedor, Ahio, Zecher, [32] and Mikloth (he fathered Shimeah). Now these also lived opposite their kinsmen in Jerusalem, with their kinsmen. [33] Ner was the father of Kish, Kish of Saul, Saul of Jonathan, Malchi-shua, Abinadab and Eshbaal; [34] and the son of Jonathan was Merib-baal; and Merib-baal was the father of Micah. [35] The sons of Micah: Pithon, Melech, Tarea, and Ahaz. [36] Ahaz fathered Jehoaddah, and Jehoaddah fathered Alemeth, Azmaveth, and Zimri. Zimri fathered Moza. [37] Moza fathered Binea; Raphah was his son, Eleasah his son, Azel his son. [38] Azel had six sons, and these are their names: Azrikam, Bocheru, Ishmael, Sheariah, Obadiah, and Hanan. All these were the sons of Azel. [39] The sons of Eshek his brother: Ulam his firstborn, Jeush the second, and Eliphelet the third. [40] The sons of Ulam were men who were mighty

warriors, bowmen, having many sons and grandsons, 150. All these were Benjaminites.

A Genealogy of the Returned Exiles

9 So all Israel was recorded in genealogies, and these are written in the Book of the Kings of Israel. And Judah was taken into exile in Babylon because of their breach of faith. ²Now the first to dwell again in their possessions in their cities were Israel, the priests, the Levites, and the temple servants. ³And some of the people of Judah, Benjamin, Ephraim, and Manasseh lived in Jerusalem: ⁴Uthai the son of Ammihud, son of Omri, son of Imri, son of Bani, from the sons of Perez the son of Judah. ⁵And of the Shilonites: Asaiah the firstborn, and his sons. ⁶Of the sons of Zerah: Jeuel and their kinsmen, 690. ⁷Of the Benjaminites: Sallu the son of Meshullam, son of Hodaviah, son of Hassenuah, ⁸Ibneiah the son of Jeroham, Elah the son of Uzzi, son of Michri, and Meshullam the son of Shephatiah, son of Reuel, son of Ibnijah; ⁹and their kinsmen according to their generations, 956. All these were heads of fathers' houses according to their fathers' houses.

¹⁰Of the priests: Jedaiah, Jehoiarib, Jachin, ¹¹and Azariah the son of Hilkiah, son of Meshullam, son of Zadok, son of Meraioth, son of Ahitub, the chief officer of the house of God; ¹²and Adaiah the son of Jeroham, son of Pashhur, son of Malchijah, and Maasai the son of Adiel, son of Jahzerah, son of Meshullam, son of Meshillemith, son of Immer; ¹³besides their kinsmen, heads of their fathers' houses, 1,760, mighty men for the work of the service of the house of God.

¹⁴Of the Levites: Shemaiah the son of Hasshub, son of Azrikam, son of Hashabiah, of the sons of Merari; ¹⁵and

Bakbakkar, Heresh, Galal and Mattaniah the son of Mica, son of Zichri, son of Asaph; ¹⁶ and Obadiah the son of Shemaiah, son of Galal, son of Jeduthun, and Berechiah the son of Asa, son of Elkanah, who lived in the villages of the Netophathites.

¹⁷ The gatekeepers were Shallum, Akkub, Talmon, Ahiman, and their kinsmen (Shallum was the chief); ¹⁸ until then they were in the king's gate on the east side as the gatekeepers of the camps of the Levites. ¹⁹ Shallum the son of Kore, son of Ebiasaph, son of Korah, and his kinsmen of his fathers' house, the Korahites, were in charge of the work of the service, keepers of the thresholds of the tent, as their fathers had been in charge of the camp of the LORD, keepers of the entrance. ²⁰ And Phinehas the son of Eleazar was the chief officer over them in time past; the LORD was with him. ²¹ Zechariah the son of Meshelemiah was gatekeeper at the entrance of the tent of meeting. ²² All these, who were chosen as gatekeepers at the thresholds, were 212. They were enrolled by genealogies in their villages. David and Samuel the seer established them in their office of trust. ²³ So they and their sons were in charge of the gates of the house of the LORD, that is, the house of the tent, as guards. ²⁴ The gatekeepers were on the four sides, east, west, north, and south. ²⁵ And their kinsmen who were in their villages were obligated to come in every seven days, in turn, to be with these, ²⁶ for the four chief gatekeepers, who were Levites, were entrusted to be over the chambers and the treasures of the house of God. ²⁷ And they lodged around the house of God, for on them lay the duty of watching, and they had charge of opening it every morning.

²⁸ Some of them had charge of the utensils of service, for they were required to count them when they were brought in and

taken out. ²⁹ Others of them were appointed over the furniture and over all the holy utensils, also over the fine flour, the wine, the oil, the incense, and the spices. ³⁰ Others, of the sons of the priests, prepared the mixing of the spices, ³¹ and Mattithiah, one of the Levites, the firstborn of Shallum the Korahite, was entrusted with making the flat cakes. ³² Also some of their kinsmen of the Kohathites had charge of the showbread, to prepare it every Sabbath.

³³ Now these, the singers, the heads of fathers' houses of the Levites, were in the chambers of the temple free from other service, for they were on duty day and night. ³⁴ These were heads of fathers' houses of the Levites, according to their generations, leaders. These lived in Jerusalem.

Saul's Genealogy Repeated

³⁵ In Gibeon lived the father of Gibeon, Jeiel, and the name of his wife was Maacah, ³⁶ and his firstborn son Abdon, then Zur, Kish, Baal, Ner, Nadab, ³⁷ Gedor, Ahio, Zechariah, and Mikloth; ³⁸ and Mikloth was the father of Shimeam; and these also lived opposite their kinsmen in Jerusalem, with their kinsmen. ³⁹ Ner fathered Kish, Kish fathered Saul, Saul fathered Jonathan, Malchi-shua, Abinadab, and Eshbaal. ⁴⁰ And the son of Jonathan was Merib-baal, and Merib-baal fathered Micah. ⁴¹ The sons of Micah: Pithon, Melech, Tahrea, and Ahaz. ⁴² And Ahaz fathered Jarah, and Jarah fathered Alemeth, Azmaveth, and Zimri. And Zimri fathered Moza. ⁴³ Moza fathered Binea, and Rephaiah was his son, Eleasah his son, Azel his son. ⁴⁴ Azel had six sons and these are their names: Azrikam, Bocheru, Ishmael, Sheariah, Obadiah, and Hanan; these were the sons of Azel.

The Death of Saul and His Sons

10 Now the Philistines fought against Israel, and the men of Israel fled before the Philistines and fell slain on Mount Gilboa. ²And the Philistines overtook Saul and his sons, and the Philistines struck down Jonathan and Abinadab and Malchi-shua, the sons of Saul. ³The battle pressed hard against Saul, and the archers found him, and he was wounded by the archers. ⁴Then Saul said to his armor-bearer, "Draw your sword and thrust me through with it, lest these uncircumcised come and mistreat me." But his armor-bearer would not, for he feared greatly. Therefore Saul took his own sword and fell upon it. ⁵And when his armor-bearer saw that Saul was dead, he also fell upon his sword and died. ⁶Thus Saul died; he and his three sons and all his house died together. ⁷And when all the men of Israel who were in the valley saw that the army had fled and that Saul and his sons were dead, they abandoned their cities and fled, and the Philistines came and lived in them.

⁸The next day, when the Philistines came to strip the slain, they found Saul and his sons fallen on Mount Gilboa. ⁹And they stripped him and took his head and his armor, and sent messengers throughout the land of the Philistines to carry the good news to their idols and to the people. ¹⁰And they put his armor in the temple of their gods and fastened his head in the temple of Dagon. ¹¹But when all Jabesh-gilead heard all that the Philistines had done to Saul, ¹²all the valiant men arose and took away the body of Saul and the bodies of his sons, and brought them to Jabesh. And they buried their bones under the oak in Jabesh and fasted seven days.

¹³ So Saul died for his breach of faith. He broke faith with the LORD in that he did not keep the command of the LORD, and also consulted a medium, seeking guidance. ¹⁴ He did not seek guidance from the LORD. Therefore the LORD put him to death and turned the kingdom over to David the son of Jesse.

David Anointed King

11 Then all Israel gathered together to David at Hebron and said, "Behold, we are your bone and flesh. ² In times past, even when Saul was king, it was you who led out and brought in Israel. And the LORD your God said to you, 'You shall be shepherd of my people Israel, and you shall be prince over my people Israel.'" ³ So all the elders of Israel came to the king at Hebron, and David made a covenant with them at Hebron before the LORD. And they anointed David king over Israel, according to the word of the LORD by Samuel.

David Takes Jerusalem

⁴ And David and all Israel went to Jerusalem, that is, Jebus, where the Jebusites were, the inhabitants of the land. ⁵ The inhabitants of Jebus said to David, "You will not come in here." Nevertheless, David took the stronghold of Zion, that is, the city of David. ⁶ David said, "Whoever strikes the Jebusites first shall be chief and commander." And Joab the son of Zeruiah went up first, so he became chief. ⁷ And David lived in the stronghold; therefore it was called the city of David. ⁸ And he built the city all around from the Millo in complete circuit, and Joab repaired the rest of the city. ⁹ And David became greater and greater, for the LORD of hosts was with him.

David's Mighty Men

¹⁰ Now these are the chiefs of David's mighty men, who gave him strong support in his kingdom, together with all Israel, to make him king, according to the word of the LORD concerning Israel. ¹¹ This is an account of David's mighty men: Jashobeam, a Hachmonite, was chief of the three. He wielded his spear against 300 whom he killed at one time.

¹² And next to him among the three mighty men was Eleazar the son of Dodo, the Ahohite. ¹³ He was with David at Pasdammim when the Philistines were gathered there for battle. There was a plot of ground full of barley, and the men fled from the Philistines. ¹⁴ But he took his stand in the midst of the plot and defended it and killed the Philistines. And the LORD saved them by a great victory.

¹⁵ Three of the thirty chief men went down to the rock to David at the cave of Adullam, when the army of Philistines was encamped in the Valley of Rephaim. ¹⁶ David was then in the stronghold, and the garrison of the Philistines was then at Bethlehem. ¹⁷ And David said longingly, "Oh that someone would give me water to drink from the well of Bethlehem that is by the gate!" ¹⁸ Then the three mighty men broke through the camp of the Philistines and drew water out of the well of Bethlehem that was by the gate and took it and brought it to David. But David would not drink it. He poured it out to the LORD ¹⁹ and said, "Far be it from me before my God that I should do this. Shall I drink the lifeblood of these men? For at the risk of their lives they brought it." Therefore he would not drink it. These things did the three mighty men.

²⁰ Now Abishai, the brother of Joab, was chief of the thirty. And he wielded his spear against 300 men and killed them and

won a name beside the three. ²¹ He was the most renowned of the thirty and became their commander, but he did not attain to the three.

²² And Benaiah the son of Jehoiada was a valiant man of Kabzeel, a doer of great deeds. He struck down two heroes of Moab. He also went down and struck down a lion in a pit on a day when snow had fallen. ²³ And he struck down an Egyptian, a man of great stature, five cubits tall. The Egyptian had in his hand a spear like a weaver's beam, but Benaiah went down to him with a staff and snatched the spear out of the Egyptian's hand and killed him with his own spear. ²⁴ These things did Benaiah the son of Jehoiada and won a name beside the three mighty men. ²⁵ He was renowned among the thirty, but he did not attain to the three. And David set him over his bodyguard.

²⁶ The mighty men were Asahel the brother of Joab, Elhanan the son of Dodo of Bethlehem, ²⁷ Shammoth of Harod, Helez the Pelonite, ²⁸ Ira the son of Ikkesh of Tekoa, Abiezer of Anathoth, ²⁹ Sibbecai the Hushathite, Ilai the Ahohite, ³⁰ Maharai of Netophah, Heled the son of Baanah of Netophah, ³¹ Ithai the son of Ribai of Gibeah of the people of Benjamin, Benaiah of Pirathon, ³² Hurai of the brooks of Gaash, Abiel the Arbathite, ³³ Azmaveth of Baharum, Eliahba the Shaalbonite, ³⁴ Hashem the Gizonite, Jonathan the son of Shagee the Hararite, ³⁵ Ahiam the son of Sachar the Hararite, Eliphal the son of Ur, ³⁶ Hepher the Mecherathite, Ahijah the Pelonite, ³⁷ Hezro of Carmel, Naarai the son of Ezbai, ³⁸ Joel the brother of Nathan, Mibhar the son of Hagri, ³⁹ Zelek the Ammonite, Naharai of Beeroth, the armor-bearer of Joab the son of Zeruiah, ⁴⁰ Ira the Ithrite, Gareb the Ithrite, ⁴¹ Uriah the Hittite, Zabad the son of Ahlai, ⁴² Adina the son of Shiza the Reubenite, a leader of the

Reubenites, and thirty with him, ⁴³ Hanan the son of Maacah, and Joshaphat the Mithnite, ⁴⁴ Uzzia the Ashterathite, Shama and Jeiel the sons of Hotham the Aroerite, ⁴⁵ Jediael the son of Shimri, and Joha his brother, the Tizite, ⁴⁶ Eliel the Mahavite, and Jeribai, and Joshaviah, the sons of Elnaam, and Ithmah the Moabite, ⁴⁷ Eliel, and Obed, and Jaasiel the Mezobaite.

The Mighty Men Join David

12 Now these are the men who came to David at Ziklag, while he could not move about freely because of Saul the son of Kish. And they were among the mighty men who helped him in war. ² They were bowmen and could shoot arrows and sling stones with either the right or the left hand; they were Benjaminites, Saul's kinsmen. ³ The chief was Ahiezer, then Joash, both sons of Shemaah of Gibeah; also Jeziel and Pelet, the sons of Azmaveth; Beracah, Jehu of Anathoth, ⁴ Ishmaiah of Gibeon, a mighty man among the thirty and a leader over the thirty; Jeremiah, Jahaziel, Johanan, Jozabad of Gederah, ⁵ Eluzai, Jerimoth, Bealiah, Shemariah, Shephatiah the Haruphite; ⁶ Elkanah, Isshiah, Azarel, Joezer, and Jashobeam, the Korahites; ⁷ And Joelah and Zebadiah, the sons of Jeroham of Gedor.

⁸ From the Gadites there went over to David at the stronghold in the wilderness mighty and experienced warriors, expert with shield and spear, whose faces were like the faces of lions and who were swift as gazelles upon the mountains: ⁹ Ezer the chief, Obadiah second, Eliab third, ¹⁰ Mishmannah fourth, Jeremiah fifth, ¹¹ Attai sixth, Eliel seventh, ¹² Johanan eighth, Elzabad ninth, ¹³ Jeremiah tenth, Machbannai eleventh. ¹⁴ These Gadites were officers of the army; the least was a match for a hundred men and the greatest for a thousand. ¹⁵ These are the

men who crossed the Jordan in the first month, when it was overflowing all its banks, and put to flight all those in the valleys, to the east and to the west.

¹⁶ And some of the men of Benjamin and Judah came to the stronghold to David. ¹⁷ David went out to meet them and said to them, "If you have come to me in friendship to help me, my heart will be joined to you; but if to betray me to my adversaries, although there is no wrong in my hands, then may the God of our fathers see and rebuke you." ¹⁸ Then the Spirit clothed Amasai, chief of the thirty, and he said,

> "We are yours, O David,
>   and with you, O son of Jesse!
>   Peace, peace to you,
>   and peace to your helpers!
>   For your God helps you."

Then David received them and made them officers of his troops.

¹⁹ Some of the men of Manasseh deserted to David when he came with the Philistines for the battle against Saul. (Yet he did not help them, for the rulers of the Philistines took counsel and sent him away, saying, "At peril to our heads he will desert to his master Saul.") ²⁰ As he went to Ziklag, these men of Manasseh deserted to him: Adnah, Jozabad, Jediael, Michael, Jozabad, Elihu, and Zillethai, chiefs of thousands in Manasseh. ²¹ They helped David against the band of raiders, for they were all mighty men of valor and were commanders in the army. ²² For from day to day men came to David to help him, until there was a great army, like an army of God.

²³ These are the numbers of the divisions of the armed troops who came to David in Hebron to turn the kingdom of Saul over to him, according to the word of the LORD. ²⁴ The men of Judah bearing shield and spear were 6,800 armed troops. ²⁵ Of the Simeonites, mighty men of valor for war, 7,100. ²⁶ Of the Levites 4,600. ²⁷ The prince Jehoiada, of the house of Aaron, and with him 3,700. ²⁸ Zadok, a young man mighty in valor, and twenty-two commanders from his own fathers' house. ²⁹ Of the Benjaminites, the kinsmen of Saul, 3,000, of whom the majority had to that point kept their allegiance to the house of Saul. ³⁰ Of the Ephraimites 20,800, mighty men of valor, famous men in their fathers' houses. ³¹ Of the half-tribe of Manasseh 18,000, who were expressly named to come and make David king. ³² Of Issachar, men who had understanding of the times, to know what Israel ought to do, 200 chiefs, and all their kinsmen under their command. ³³ Of Zebulun 50,000 seasoned troops, equipped for battle with all the weapons of war, to help David with singleness of purpose. ³⁴ Of Naphtali 1,000 commanders with whom were 37,000 men armed with shield and spear. ³⁵ Of the Danites 28,600 men equipped for battle. ³⁶ Of Asher 40,000 seasoned troops ready for battle. ³⁷ Of the Reubenites and Gadites and the half-tribe of Manasseh from beyond the Jordan, 120,000 men armed with all the weapons of war.

³⁸ All these, men of war, arrayed in battle order, came to Hebron with a whole heart to make David king over all Israel. Likewise, all the rest of Israel were of a single mind to make David king. ³⁹ And they were there with David for three days, eating and drinking, for their brothers had made preparation for them. ⁴⁰ And also their relatives, from as far as Issachar and Zebulun and Naphtali, came bringing food on donkeys and

on camels and on mules and on oxen, abundant provisions of flour, cakes of figs, clusters of raisins, and wine and oil, oxen and sheep, for there was joy in Israel.

The Ark Brought from Kiriath-Jearim

13 David consulted with the commanders of thousands and of hundreds, with every leader. ² And David said to all the assembly of Israel, "If it seems good to you and from the LORD our God, let us send abroad to our brothers who remain in all the lands of Israel, as well as to the priests and Levites in the cities that have pasturelands, that they may be gathered to us. ³ Then let us bring again the ark of our God to us, for we did not seek it in the days of Saul." ⁴ All the assembly agreed to do so, for the thing was right in the eyes of all the people.

Uzzah and the Ark

⁵ So David assembled all Israel from the Nile of Egypt to Lebo-hamath, to bring the ark of God from Kiriath-jearim. ⁶ And David and all Israel went up to Baalah, that is, to Kiriath-jearim that belongs to Judah, to bring up from there the ark of God, which is called by the name of the LORD who sits enthroned above the cherubim. ⁷ And they carried the ark of God on a new cart, from the house of Abinadab, and Uzzah and Ahio were driving the cart. ⁸ And David and all Israel were celebrating before God with all their might, with song and lyres and harps and tambourines and cymbals and trumpets.

⁹ And when they came to the threshing floor of Chidon, Uzzah put out his hand to take hold of the ark, for the oxen stumbled. ¹⁰ And the anger of the LORD was kindled against Uzzah, and he struck him down because he put out his hand to

the ark, and he died there before God. ¹¹ And David was angry because the Lᴏʀᴅ had broken out against Uzzah. And that place is called Perez-uzza to this day. ¹² And David was afraid of God that day, and he said, "How can I bring the ark of God home to me?" ¹³ So David did not take the ark home into the city of David, but took it aside to the house of Obed-edom the Gittite. ¹⁴ And the ark of God remained with the household of Obed-edom in his house three months. And the Lᴏʀᴅ blessed the household of Obed-edom and all that he had.

David's Wives and Children

14 And Hiram king of Tyre sent messengers to David, and cedar trees, also masons and carpenters to build a house for him. ² And David knew that the Lᴏʀᴅ had established him as king over Israel, and that his kingdom was highly exalted for the sake of his people Israel.

³ And David took more wives in Jerusalem, and David fathered more sons and daughters. ⁴ These are the names of the children born to him in Jerusalem: Shammua, Shobab, Nathan, Solomon, ⁵ Ibhar, Elishua, Elpelet, ⁶ Nogah, Nepheg, Japhia, ⁷ Elishama, Beeliada and Eliphelet.

Philistines Defeated

⁸ When the Philistines heard that David had been anointed king over all Israel, all the Philistines went up to search for David. But David heard of it and went out against them. ⁹ Now the Philistines had come and made a raid in the Valley of Rephaim. ¹⁰ And David inquired of God, "Shall I go up against the Philistines? Will you give them into my hand?" And the Lᴏʀᴅ said to him, "Go up, and I will give them into your

hand." ¹¹ And he went up to Baal-perazim, and David struck them down there. And David said, "God has broken through my enemies by my hand, like a bursting flood." Therefore the name of that place is called Baal-perazim. ¹² And they left their gods there, and David gave command, and they were burned.

¹³ And the Philistines yet again made a raid in the valley. ¹⁴ And when David again inquired of God, God said to him, "You shall not go up after them; go around and come against them opposite the balsam trees. ¹⁵ And when you hear the sound of marching in the tops of the balsam trees, then go out to battle, for God has gone out before you to strike down the army of the Philistines." ¹⁶ And David did as God commanded him, and they struck down the Philistine army from Gibeon to Gezer. ¹⁷ And the fame of David went out into all lands, and the LORD brought the fear of him upon all nations.

The Ark Brought to Jerusalem

15 David built houses for himself in the city of David. And he prepared a place for the ark of God and pitched a tent for it. ² Then David said that no one but the Levites may carry the ark of God, for the LORD had chosen them to carry the ark of the LORD and to minister to him forever. ³ And David assembled all Israel at Jerusalem to bring up the ark of the LORD to its place, which he had prepared for it. ⁴ And David gathered together the sons of Aaron and the Levites: ⁵ of the sons of Kohath, Uriel the chief, with 120 of his brothers; ⁶ of the sons of Merari, Asaiah the chief, with 220 of his brothers; ⁷ of the sons of Gershom, Joel the chief, with 130 of his brothers; ⁸ of the sons of Elizaphan, Shemaiah the chief, with 200 of his brothers; ⁹ of the sons of Hebron, Eliel the chief, with 80 of his brothers; ¹⁰ of the sons of

Uzziel, Amminadab the chief, with 112 of his brothers. ¹¹ Then David summoned the priests Zadok and Abiathar, and the Levites Uriel, Asaiah, Joel, Shemaiah, Eliel, and Amminadab, ¹² and said to them, "You are the heads of the fathers' houses of the Levites. Consecrate yourselves, you and your brothers, so that you may bring up the ark of the Lord, the God of Israel, to the place that I have prepared for it. ¹³ Because you did not carry it the first time, the Lord our God broke out against us, because we did not seek him according to the rule." ¹⁴ So the priests and the Levites consecrated themselves to bring up the ark of the Lord, the God of Israel. ¹⁵ And the Levites carried the ark of God on their shoulders with the poles, as Moses had commanded according to the word of the Lord.

¹⁶ David also commanded the chiefs of the Levites to appoint their brothers as the singers who should play loudly on musical instruments, on harps and lyres and cymbals, to raise sounds of joy. ¹⁷ So the Levites appointed Heman the son of Joel; and of his brothers Asaph the son of Berechiah; and of the sons of Merari, their brothers, Ethan the son of Kushaiah; ¹⁸ and with them their brothers of the second order, Zechariah, Jaaziel, Shemiramoth, Jehiel, Unni, Eliab, Benaiah, Maaseiah, Mattithiah, Eliphelehu, and Mikneiah, and the gatekeepers Obed-edom and Jeiel. ¹⁹ The singers, Heman, Asaph, and Ethan, were to sound bronze cymbals; ²⁰ Zechariah, Aziel, Shemiramoth, Jehiel, Unni, Eliab, Maaseiah, and Benaiah were to play harps according to Alamoth; ²¹ but Mattithiah, Eliphelehu, Mikneiah, Obed-edom, Jeiel, and Azaziah were to lead with lyres according to the Sheminith. ²² Chenaniah, leader of the Levites in music, should direct the music, for he understood it. ²³ Berechiah and Elkanah were to be gatekeepers

for the ark. ²⁴ Shebaniah, Joshaphat, Nethanel, Amasai, Zechariah, Benaiah, and Eliezer, the priests, should blow the trumpets before the ark of God. Obed-edom and Jehiah were to be gatekeepers for the ark.

²⁵ So David and the elders of Israel and the commanders of thousands went to bring up the ark of the covenant of the LORD from the house of Obed-edom with rejoicing. ²⁶ And because God helped the Levites who were carrying the ark of the covenant of the LORD, they sacrificed seven bulls and seven rams. ²⁷ David was clothed with a robe of fine linen, as also were all the Levites who were carrying the ark, and the singers and Chenaniah the leader of the music of the singers. And David wore a linen ephod. ²⁸ So all Israel brought up the ark of the covenant of the LORD with shouting, to the sound of the horn, trumpets, and cymbals, and made loud music on harps and lyres.

²⁹ And as the ark of the covenant of the LORD came to the city of David, Michal the daughter of Saul looked out of the window and saw King David dancing and celebrating, and she despised him in her heart.

The Ark Placed in a Tent

16 And they brought in the ark of God and set it inside the tent that David had pitched for it, and they offered burnt offerings and peace offerings before God. ² And when David had finished offering the burnt offerings and the peace offerings, he blessed the people in the name of the LORD ³ and distributed to all Israel, both men and women, to each a loaf of bread, a portion of meat, and a cake of raisins.

⁴ Then he appointed some of the Levites as ministers before the ark of the LORD, to invoke, to thank, and to praise the

LORD, the God of Israel. ⁵Asaph was the chief, and second to him were Zechariah, Jeiel, Shemiramoth, Jehiel, Mattithiah, Eliab, Benaiah, Obed-edom, and Jeiel, who were to play harps and lyres; Asaph was to sound the cymbals, ⁶and Benaiah and Jahaziel the priests were to blow trumpets regularly before the ark of the covenant of God. ⁷Then on that day David first appointed that thanksgiving be sung to the LORD by Asaph and his brothers.

David's Song of Thanks

⁸   Oh give thanks to the LORD; call upon his name;
       make known his deeds among the peoples!
⁹   Sing to him, sing praises to him;
       tell of all his wondrous works!
¹⁰   Glory in his holy name;
       let the hearts of those who seek the LORD rejoice!
¹¹   Seek the LORD and his strength;
       seek his presence continually!
¹²   Remember the wondrous works that he has done,
       his miracles and the judgments he uttered,
¹³   O offspring of Israel his servant,
       children of Jacob, his chosen ones!

¹⁴   He is the LORD our God;
       his judgments are in all the earth.
¹⁵   Remember his covenant forever,
       the word that he commanded, for a thousand
          generations,
¹⁶   the covenant that he made with Abraham,
       his sworn promise to Isaac,

¹⁷ which he confirmed to Jacob as a statute,
  to Israel as an everlasting covenant,
¹⁸ saying, "To you I will give the land of Canaan,
  as your portion for an inheritance."

¹⁹ When you were few in number,
  of little account, and sojourners in it,
²⁰ wandering from nation to nation,
  from one kingdom to another people,
²¹ he allowed no one to oppress them;
  he rebuked kings on their account,
²² saying, "Touch not my anointed ones,
  do my prophets no harm!"

²³ Sing to the LORD, all the earth!
  Tell of his salvation from day to day.
²⁴ Declare his glory among the nations,
  his marvelous works among all the peoples!
²⁵ For great is the LORD, and greatly to be praised,
  and he is to be feared above all gods.
²⁶ For all the gods of the peoples are worthless
    idols,
  but the LORD made the heavens.
²⁷ Splendor and majesty are before him;
  strength and joy are in his place.

²⁸ Ascribe to the LORD, O families of the peoples,
  ascribe to the LORD glory and strength!
²⁹ Ascribe to the LORD the glory due his name;
  bring an offering and come before him!

> Worship the Lord in the splendor of holiness;
> 30 tremble before him, all the earth;
>   yes, the world is established; it shall never be
>   moved.
> 31 Let the heavens be glad, and let the earth rejoice,
>   and let them say among the nations, "The Lord
>   reigns!"
> 32 Let the sea roar, and all that fills it;
>   let the field exult, and everything in it!
> 33 Then shall the trees of the forest sing for joy
>   before the Lord, for he comes to judge the earth.
> 34 Oh give thanks to the Lord, for he is good;
>   for his steadfast love endures forever!

³⁵ Say also:

> "Save us, O God of our salvation,
>   and gather and deliver us from among the nations,
>   that we may give thanks to your holy name
>   and glory in your praise.
> 36 Blessed be the Lord, the God of Israel,
>   from everlasting to everlasting!"

Then all the people said, "Amen!" and praised the Lord.

Worship Before the Ark

³⁷ So David left Asaph and his brothers there before the ark of the covenant of the Lord to minister regularly before the ark as each day required, ³⁸ and also Obed-edom and his sixty-eight brothers, while Obed-edom, the son of Jeduthun, and

Hosah were to be gatekeepers. ³⁹ And he left Zadok the priest and his brothers the priests before the tabernacle of the Lord in the high place that was at Gibeon ⁴⁰ to offer burnt offerings to the Lord on the altar of burnt offering regularly morning and evening, to do all that is written in the Law of the Lord that he commanded Israel. ⁴¹ With them were Heman and Jeduthun and the rest of those chosen and expressly named to give thanks to the Lord, for his steadfast love endures forever. ⁴² Heman and Jeduthun had trumpets and cymbals for the music and instruments for sacred song. The sons of Jeduthun were appointed to the gate.

⁴³ Then all the people departed each to his house, and David went home to bless his household.

The Lord's Covenant with David

17 Now when David lived in his house, David said to Nathan the prophet, "Behold, I dwell in a house of cedar, but the ark of the covenant of the Lord is under a tent." ² And Nathan said to David, "Do all that is in your heart, for God is with you."

³ But that same night the word of the Lord came to Nathan, ⁴ "Go and tell my servant David, 'Thus says the Lord: It is not you who will build me a house to dwell in. ⁵ For I have not lived in a house since the day I brought up Israel to this day, but I have gone from tent to tent and from dwelling to dwelling. ⁶ In all places where I have moved with all Israel, did I speak a word with any of the judges of Israel, whom I commanded to shepherd my people, saying, "Why have you not built me a house of cedar?"' ⁷ Now, therefore, thus shall you say to my servant David, 'Thus says the Lord of hosts, I took you from the

pasture, from following the sheep, to be prince over my people Israel, ⁸ and I have been with you wherever you have gone and have cut off all your enemies from before you. And I will make for you a name, like the name of the great ones of the earth. ⁹ And I will appoint a place for my people Israel and will plant them, that they may dwell in their own place and be disturbed no more. And violent men shall waste them no more, as formerly, ¹⁰ from the time that I appointed judges over my people Israel. And I will subdue all your enemies. Moreover, I declare to you that the LORD will build you a house. ¹¹ When your days are fulfilled to walk with your fathers, I will raise up your offspring after you, one of your own sons, and I will establish his kingdom. ¹² He shall build a house for me, and I will establish his throne forever. ¹³ I will be to him a father, and he shall be to me a son. I will not take my steadfast love from him, as I took it from him who was before you, ¹⁴ but I will confirm him in my house and in my kingdom forever, and his throne shall be established forever.'" ¹⁵ In accordance with all these words, and in accordance with all this vision, Nathan spoke to David.

David's Prayer

¹⁶ Then King David went in and sat before the LORD and said, "Who am I, O LORD God, and what is my house, that you have brought me thus far? ¹⁷ And this was a small thing in your eyes, O God. You have also spoken of your servant's house for a great while to come, and have shown me future generations, O LORD God! ¹⁸ And what more can David say to you for honoring your servant? For you know your servant. ¹⁹ For your servant's sake, O LORD, and according to your own heart, you have done all this greatness, in making known all these great things.

²⁰ There is none like you, O Lord, and there is no God besides you, according to all that we have heard with our ears. ²¹ And who is like your people Israel, the one nation on earth whom God went to redeem to be his people, making for yourself a name for great and awesome things, in driving out nations before your people whom you redeemed from Egypt? ²² And you made your people Israel to be your people forever, and you, O Lord, became their God. ²³ And now, O Lord, let the word that you have spoken concerning your servant and concerning his house be established forever, and do as you have spoken, ²⁴ and your name will be established and magnified forever, saying, 'The Lord of hosts, the God of Israel, is Israel's God,' and the house of your servant David will be established before you. ²⁵ For you, my God, have revealed to your servant that you will build a house for him. Therefore your servant has found courage to pray before you. ²⁶ And now, O Lord, you are God, and you have promised this good thing to your servant. ²⁷ Now you have been pleased to bless the house of your servant, that it may continue forever before you, for it is you, O Lord, who have blessed, and it is blessed forever."

David Defeats His Enemies

18 After this David defeated the Philistines and subdued them, and he took Gath and its villages out of the hand of the Philistines.

² And he defeated Moab, and the Moabites became servants to David and brought tribute.

³ David also defeated Hadadezer king of Zobah-Hamath, as he went to set up his monument at the river Euphrates. ⁴ And David took from him 1,000 chariots, 7,000 horsemen,

and 20,000 foot soldiers. And David hamstrung all the chariot horses, but left enough for 100 chariots. ⁵And when the Syrians of Damascus came to help Hadadezer king of Zobah, David struck down 22,000 men of the Syrians. ⁶Then David put garrisons in Syria of Damascus, and the Syrians became servants to David and brought tribute. And the Lᴏʀᴅ gave victory to David wherever he went. ⁷And David took the shields of gold that were carried by the servants of Hadadezer and brought them to Jerusalem. ⁸And from Tibhath and from Cun, cities of Hadadezer, David took a large amount of bronze. With it Solomon made the bronze sea and the pillars and the vessels of bronze.

⁹When Tou king of Hamath heard that David had defeated the whole army of Hadadezer, king of Zobah, ¹⁰he sent his son Hadoram to King David, to ask about his health and to bless him because he had fought against Hadadezer and defeated him; for Hadadezer had often been at war with Tou. And he sent all sorts of articles of gold, of silver, and of bronze. ¹¹These also King David dedicated to the Lᴏʀᴅ, together with the silver and gold that he had carried off from all the nations, from Edom, Moab, the Ammonites, the Philistines, and Amalek.

¹²And Abishai, the son of Zeruiah, killed 18,000 Edomites in the Valley of Salt. ¹³Then he put garrisons in Edom, and all the Edomites became David's servants. And the Lᴏʀᴅ gave victory to David wherever he went.

David's Administration

¹⁴So David reigned over all Israel, and he administered justice and equity to all his people. ¹⁵And Joab the son of Zeruiah was over the army; and Jehoshaphat the son of Ahilud was

recorder; [16] and Zadok the son of Ahitub and Ahimelech the son of Abiathar were priests; and Shavsha was secretary; [17] and Benaiah the son of Jehoiada was over the Cherethites and the Pelethites; and David's sons were the chief officials in the service of the king.

The Ammonites Disgrace David's Men

19 Now after this Nahash the king of the Ammonites died, and his son reigned in his place. [2] And David said, "I will deal kindly with Hanun the son of Nahash, for his father dealt kindly with me." So David sent messengers to console him concerning his father. And David's servants came to the land of the Ammonites to Hanun to console him. [3] But the princes of the Ammonites said to Hanun, "Do you think, because David has sent comforters to you, that he is honoring your father? Have not his servants come to you to search and to overthrow and to spy out the land?" [4] So Hanun took David's servants and shaved them and cut off their garments in the middle, at their hips, and sent them away; [5] and they departed. When David was told concerning the men, he sent messengers to meet them, for the men were greatly ashamed. And the king said, "Remain at Jericho until your beards have grown and then return."

[6] When the Ammonites saw that they had become a stench to David, Hanun and the Ammonites sent 1,000 talents of silver to hire chariots and horsemen from Mesopotamia, from Aram-maacah, and from Zobah. [7] They hired 32,000 chariots and the king of Maacah with his army, who came and encamped before Medeba. And the Ammonites were mustered from their cities and came to battle. [8] When David heard of it, he sent Joab and all the army of the mighty men. [9] And

the Ammonites came out and drew up in battle array at the entrance of the city, and the kings who had come were by themselves in the open country.

Ammonites and Syrians Defeated

¹⁰When Joab saw that the battle was set against him both in front and in the rear, he chose some of the best men of Israel and arrayed them against the Syrians. ¹¹The rest of his men he put in the charge of Abishai his brother, and they were arrayed against the Ammonites. ¹²And he said, "If the Syrians are too strong for me, then you shall help me, but if the Ammonites are too strong for you, then I will help you. ¹³Be strong, and let us use our strength for our people and for the cities of our God, and may the LORD do what seems good to him." ¹⁴So Joab and the people who were with him drew near before the Syrians for battle, and they fled before him. ¹⁵And when the Ammonites saw that the Syrians fled, they likewise fled before Abishai, Joab's brother, and entered the city. Then Joab came to Jerusalem.

¹⁶But when the Syrians saw that they had been defeated by Israel, they sent messengers and brought out the Syrians who were beyond the Euphrates, with Shophach the commander of the army of Hadadezer at their head. ¹⁷And when it was told to David, he gathered all Israel together and crossed the Jordan and came to them and drew up his forces against them. And when David set the battle in array against the Syrians, they fought with him. ¹⁸And the Syrians fled before Israel, and David killed of the Syrians the men of 7,000 chariots and 40,000 foot soldiers, and put to death also Shophach the commander of their army. ¹⁹And when the servants of Hadadezer saw that

they had been defeated by Israel, they made peace with David and became subject to him. So the Syrians were not willing to save the Ammonites anymore.

The Capture of Rabbah

20 In the spring of the year, the time when kings go out to battle, Joab led out the army and ravaged the country of the Ammonites and came and besieged Rabbah. But David remained at Jerusalem. And Joab struck down Rabbah and overthrew it. ² And David took the crown of their king from his head. He found that it weighed a talent of gold, and in it was a precious stone. And it was placed on David's head. And he brought out the spoil of the city, a very great amount. ³ And he brought out the people who were in it and set them to labor with saws and iron picks and axes. And thus David did to all the cities of the Ammonites. Then David and all the people returned to Jerusalem.

Philistine Giants Killed

⁴ And after this there arose war with the Philistines at Gezer. Then Sibbecai the Hushathite struck down Sippai, who was one of the descendants of the giants, and the Philistines were subdued. ⁵ And there was again war with the Philistines, and Elhanan the son of Jair struck down Lahmi the brother of Goliath the Gittite, the shaft of whose spear was like a weaver's beam. ⁶ And there was again war at Gath, where there was a man of great stature, who had six fingers on each hand and six toes on each foot, twenty-four in number, and he also was descended from the giants. ⁷ And when he taunted Israel, Jonathan the son of Shimea, David's brother, struck him down.

⁸ These were descended from the giants in Gath, and they fell by the hand of David and by the hand of his servants.

David's Census Brings Pestilence

21 Then Satan stood against Israel and incited David to number Israel. ² So David said to Joab and the commanders of the army, "Go, number Israel, from Beersheba to Dan, and bring me a report, that I may know their number." ³ But Joab said, "May the LORD add to his people a hundred times as many as they are! Are they not, my lord the king, all of them my lord's servants? Why then should my lord require this? Why should it be a cause of guilt for Israel?" ⁴ But the king's word prevailed against Joab. So Joab departed and went throughout all Israel and came back to Jerusalem. ⁵ And Joab gave the sum of the numbering of the people to David. In all Israel there were 1,100,000 men who drew the sword, and in Judah 470,000 who drew the sword. ⁶ But he did not include Levi and Benjamin in the numbering, for the king's command was abhorrent to Joab.

⁷ But God was displeased with this thing, and he struck Israel. ⁸ And David said to God, "I have sinned greatly in that I have done this thing. But now, please take away the iniquity of your servant, for I have acted very foolishly." ⁹ And the LORD spoke to Gad, David's seer, saying, ¹⁰ "Go and say to David, 'Thus says the LORD, Three things I offer you; choose one of them, that I may do it to you.'" ¹¹ So Gad came to David and said to him, "Thus says the LORD, 'Choose what you will: ¹² either three years of famine, or three months of devastation by your foes while the sword of your enemies overtakes you, or else three days of the sword of the LORD, pestilence on the land, with the

angel of the LORD destroying throughout all the territory of Israel.' Now decide what answer I shall return to him who sent me." ¹³ Then David said to Gad, "I am in great distress. Let me fall into the hand of the LORD, for his mercy is very great, but do not let me fall into the hand of man."

¹⁴ So the LORD sent a pestilence on Israel, and 70,000 men of Israel fell. ¹⁵ And God sent the angel to Jerusalem to destroy it, but as he was about to destroy it, the LORD saw, and he relented from the calamity. And he said to the angel who was working destruction, "It is enough; now stay your hand." And the angel of the LORD was standing by the threshing floor of Ornan the Jebusite. ¹⁶ And David lifted his eyes and saw the angel of the LORD standing between earth and heaven, and in his hand a drawn sword stretched out over Jerusalem. Then David and the elders, clothed in sackcloth, fell upon their faces. ¹⁷ And David said to God, "Was it not I who gave command to number the people? It is I who have sinned and done great evil. But these sheep, what have they done? Please let your hand, O LORD my God, be against me and against my father's house. But do not let the plague be on your people."

David Builds an Altar

¹⁸ Now the angel of the LORD had commanded Gad to say to David that David should go up and raise an altar to the LORD on the threshing floor of Ornan the Jebusite. ¹⁹ So David went up at Gad's word, which he had spoken in the name of the LORD. ²⁰ Now Ornan was threshing wheat. He turned and saw the angel, and his four sons who were with him hid themselves. ²¹ As David came to Ornan, Ornan looked and saw David and went out from the threshing floor and paid homage to

David with his face to the ground. ²²And David said to Ornan, "Give me the site of the threshing floor that I may build on it an altar to the LORD—give it to me at its full price—that the plague may be averted from the people." ²³Then Ornan said to David, "Take it, and let my lord the king do what seems good to him. See, I give the oxen for burnt offerings and the threshing sledges for the wood and the wheat for a grain offering; I give it all." ²⁴But King David said to Ornan, "No, but I will buy them for the full price. I will not take for the LORD what is yours, nor offer burnt offerings that cost me nothing." ²⁵So David paid Ornan 600 shekels of gold by weight for the site. ²⁶And David built there an altar to the LORD and presented burnt offerings and peace offerings and called on the LORD, and the LORD answered him with fire from heaven upon the altar of burnt offering. ²⁷Then the LORD commanded the angel, and he put his sword back into its sheath.

²⁸At that time, when David saw that the LORD had answered him at the threshing floor of Ornan the Jebusite, he sacrificed there. ²⁹For the tabernacle of the LORD, which Moses had made in the wilderness, and the altar of burnt offering were at that time in the high place at Gibeon, ³⁰but David could not go before it to inquire of God, for he was afraid of the sword of the angel of the LORD.

22 Then David said, "Here shall be the house of the LORD God and here the altar of burnt offering for Israel."

David Prepares for Temple Building

²David commanded to gather together the resident aliens who were in the land of Israel, and he set stonecutters to prepare dressed stones for building the house of God. ³David

also provided great quantities of iron for nails for the doors of the gates and for clamps, as well as bronze in quantities beyond weighing, ⁴ and cedar timbers without number, for the Sidonians and Tyrians brought great quantities of cedar to David. ⁵ For David said, "Solomon my son is young and inexperienced, and the house that is to be built for the LORD must be exceedingly magnificent, of fame and glory throughout all lands. I will therefore make preparation for it." So David provided materials in great quantity before his death.

Solomon Charged to Build the Temple

⁶ Then he called for Solomon his son and charged him to build a house for the LORD, the God of Israel. ⁷ David said to Solomon, "My son, I had it in my heart to build a house to the name of the LORD my God. ⁸ But the word of the LORD came to me, saying, 'You have shed much blood and have waged great wars. You shall not build a house to my name, because you have shed so much blood before me on the earth. ⁹ Behold, a son shall be born to you who shall be a man of rest. I will give him rest from all his surrounding enemies. For his name shall be Solomon, and I will give peace and quiet to Israel in his days. ¹⁰ He shall build a house for my name. He shall be my son, and I will be his father, and I will establish his royal throne in Israel forever.'

¹¹ "Now, my son, the LORD be with you, so that you may succeed in building the house of the LORD your God, as he has spoken concerning you. ¹² Only, may the LORD grant you discretion and understanding, that when he gives you charge over Israel you may keep the law of the LORD your God. ¹³ Then you will prosper if you are careful to observe the statutes and the rules that the LORD commanded Moses for Israel. Be strong and

courageous. Fear not; do not be dismayed. ¹⁴With great pains I have provided for the house of the LORD 100,000 talents of gold, a million talents of silver, and bronze and iron beyond weighing, for there is so much of it; timber and stone, too, I have provided. To these you must add. ¹⁵You have an abundance of workmen: stonecutters, masons, carpenters, and all kinds of craftsmen without number, skilled in working ¹⁶gold, silver, bronze, and iron. Arise and work! The LORD be with you!"

¹⁷David also commanded all the leaders of Israel to help Solomon his son, saying, ¹⁸"Is not the LORD your God with you? And has he not given you peace on every side? For he has delivered the inhabitants of the land into my hand, and the land is subdued before the LORD and his people. ¹⁹Now set your mind and heart to seek the LORD your God. Arise and build the sanctuary of the LORD God, so that the ark of the covenant of the LORD and the holy vessels of God may be brought into a house built for the name of the LORD."

David Organizes the Levites

23 When David was old and full of days, he made Solomon his son king over Israel.

²David assembled all the leaders of Israel and the priests and the Levites. ³The Levites, thirty years old and upward, were numbered, and the total was 38,000 men. ⁴"Twenty-four thousand of these," David said, "shall have charge of the work in the house of the LORD, 6,000 shall be officers and judges, ⁵4,000 gatekeepers, and 4,000 shall offer praises to the LORD with the instruments that I have made for praise." ⁶And David organized them in divisions corresponding to the sons of Levi: Gershon, Kohath, and Merari.

[7] The sons of Gershon were Ladan and Shimei. [8] The sons of Ladan: Jehiel the chief, and Zetham, and Joel, three. [9] The sons of Shimei: Shelomoth, Haziel, and Haran, three. These were the heads of the fathers' houses of Ladan. [10] And the sons of Shimei: Jahath, Zina, and Jeush and Beriah. These four were the sons of Shimei. [11] Jahath was the chief, and Zizah the second; but Jeush and Beriah did not have many sons, therefore they became counted as a single father's house.

[12] The sons of Kohath: Amram, Izhar, Hebron, and Uzziel, four. [13] The sons of Amram: Aaron and Moses. Aaron was set apart to dedicate the most holy things, that he and his sons forever should make offerings before the LORD and minister to him and pronounce blessings in his name forever. [14] But the sons of Moses the man of God were named among the tribe of Levi. [15] The sons of Moses: Gershom and Eliezer. [16] The sons of Gershom: Shebuel the chief. [17] The sons of Eliezer: Rehabiah the chief. Eliezer had no other sons, but the sons of Rehabiah were very many. [18] The sons of Izhar: Shelomith the chief. [19] The sons of Hebron: Jeriah the chief, Amariah the second, Jahaziel the third, and Jekameam the fourth. [20] The sons of Uzziel: Micah the chief and Isshiah the second.

[21] The sons of Merari: Mahli and Mushi. The sons of Mahli: Eleazar and Kish. [22] Eleazar died having no sons, but only daughters; their kinsmen, the sons of Kish, married them. [23] The sons of Mushi: Mahli, Eder, and Jeremoth, three.

[24] These were the sons of Levi by their fathers' houses, the heads of fathers' houses as they were listed according to the number of the names of the individuals from twenty years old and upward who were to do the work for the service of the house of the LORD. [25] For David said, "The LORD, the God of

Israel, has given rest to his people, and he dwells in Jerusalem forever. ²⁶ And so the Levites no longer need to carry the tabernacle or any of the things for its service." ²⁷ For by the last words of David the sons of Levi were numbered from twenty years old and upward. ²⁸ For their duty was to assist the sons of Aaron for the service of the house of the LORD, having the care of the courts and the chambers, the cleansing of all that is holy, and any work for the service of the house of God. ²⁹ Their duty was also to assist with the showbread, the flour for the grain offering, the wafers of unleavened bread, the baked offering, the offering mixed with oil, and all measures of quantity or size. ³⁰ And they were to stand every morning, thanking and praising the LORD, and likewise at evening, ³¹ and whenever burnt offerings were offered to the LORD on Sabbaths, new moons, and feast days, according to the number required of them, regularly before the LORD. ³² Thus they were to keep charge of the tent of meeting and the sanctuary, and to attend the sons of Aaron, their brothers, for the service of the house of the LORD.

David Organizes the Priests

24 The divisions of the sons of Aaron were these. The sons of Aaron: Nadab, Abihu, Eleazar, and Ithamar. ² But Nadab and Abihu died before their father and had no children, so Eleazar and Ithamar became the priests. ³ With the help of Zadok of the sons of Eleazar, and Ahimelech of the sons of Ithamar, David organized them according to the appointed duties in their service. ⁴ Since more chief men were found among the sons of Eleazar than among the sons of Ithamar, they organized them under sixteen heads of fathers' houses of the sons of Eleazar, and eight of the sons of Ithamar.

⁵ They divided them by lot, all alike, for there were sacred officers and officers of God among both the sons of Eleazar and the sons of Ithamar. ⁶ And the scribe Shemaiah, the son of Nethanel, a Levite, recorded them in the presence of the king and the princes and Zadok the priest and Ahimelech the son of Abiathar and the heads of the fathers' houses of the priests and of the Levites, one father's house being chosen for Eleazar and one chosen for Ithamar.

⁷ The first lot fell to Jehoiarib, the second to Jedaiah, ⁸ the third to Harim, the fourth to Seorim, ⁹ the fifth to Malchijah, the sixth to Mijamin, ¹⁰ the seventh to Hakkoz, the eighth to Abijah, ¹¹ the ninth to Jeshua, the tenth to Shecaniah, ¹² the eleventh to Eliashib, the twelfth to Jakim, ¹³ the thirteenth to Huppah, the fourteenth to Jeshebeab, ¹⁴ the fifteenth to Bilgah, the sixteenth to Immer, ¹⁵ the seventeenth to Hezir, the eighteenth to Happizzez, ¹⁶ the nineteenth to Pethahiah, the twentieth to Jehezkel, ¹⁷ the twenty-first to Jachin, the twenty-second to Gamul, ¹⁸ the twenty-third to Delaiah, the twenty-fourth to Maaziah. ¹⁹ These had as their appointed duty in their service to come into the house of the LORD according to the procedure established for them by Aaron their father, as the LORD God of Israel had commanded him.

²⁰ And of the rest of the sons of Levi: of the sons of Amram, Shubael; of the sons of Shubael, Jehdeiah. ²¹ Of Rehabiah: of the sons of Rehabiah, Isshiah the chief. ²² Of the Izharites, Shelomoth; of the sons of Shelomoth, Jahath. ²³ The sons of Hebron: Jeriah the chief, Amariah the second, Jahaziel the third, Jekameam the fourth. ²⁴ The sons of Uzziel, Micah; of the sons of Micah, Shamir. ²⁵ The brother of Micah, Isshiah; of the sons of Isshiah, Zechariah. ²⁶ The sons of Merari: Mahli and Mushi.

The sons of Jaaziah: Beno. ²⁷ The sons of Merari: of Jaaziah, Beno, Shoham, Zaccur, and Ibri. ²⁸ Of Mahli: Eleazar, who had no sons. ²⁹ Of Kish, the sons of Kish: Jerahmeel. ³⁰ The sons of Mushi: Mahli, Eder, and Jerimoth. These were the sons of the Levites according to their fathers' houses. ³¹ These also, the head of each father's house and his younger brother alike, cast lots, just as their brothers the sons of Aaron, in the presence of King David, Zadok, Ahimelech, and the heads of fathers' houses of the priests and of the Levites.

David Organizes the Musicians

25 David and the chiefs of the service also set apart for the service the sons of Asaph, and of Heman, and of Jeduthun, who prophesied with lyres, with harps, and with cymbals. The list of those who did the work and of their duties was: ² Of the sons of Asaph: Zaccur, Joseph, Nethaniah, and Asharelah, sons of Asaph, under the direction of Asaph, who prophesied under the direction of the king. ³ Of Jeduthun, the sons of Jeduthun: Gedaliah, Zeri, Jeshaiah, Shimei, Hashabiah, and Mattithiah, six, under the direction of their father Jeduthun, who prophesied with the lyre in thanksgiving and praise to the Lord. ⁴ Of Heman, the sons of Heman: Bukkiah, Mattaniah, Uzziel, Shebuel and Jerimoth, Hananiah, Hanani, Eliathah, Giddalti, and Romamti-ezer, Joshbekashah, Mallothi, Hothir, Mahazioth. ⁵ All these were the sons of Heman the king's seer, according to the promise of God to exalt him, for God had given Heman fourteen sons and three daughters. ⁶ They were all under the direction of their father in the music in the house of the Lord with cymbals, harps, and lyres for the service of the house of God. Asaph,

Jeduthun, and Heman were under the order of the king. ⁷The number of them along with their brothers, who were trained in singing to the LORD, all who were skillful, was 288. ⁸And they cast lots for their duties, small and great, teacher and pupil alike.

⁹The first lot fell for Asaph to Joseph; the second to Gedaliah, to him and his brothers and his sons, twelve; ¹⁰the third to Zaccur, his sons and his brothers, twelve; ¹¹the fourth to Izri, his sons and his brothers, twelve; ¹²the fifth to Nethaniah, his sons and his brothers, twelve; ¹³the sixth to Bukkiah, his sons and his brothers, twelve; ¹⁴the seventh to Jesharelah, his sons and his brothers, twelve; ¹⁵the eighth to Jeshaiah, his sons and his brothers, twelve; ¹⁶the ninth to Mattaniah, his sons and his brothers, twelve; ¹⁷the tenth to Shimei, his sons and his brothers, twelve; ¹⁸the eleventh to Azarel, his sons and his brothers, twelve; ¹⁹the twelfth to Hashabiah, his sons and his brothers, twelve; ²⁰to the thirteenth, Shubael, his sons and his brothers, twelve; ²¹to the fourteenth, Mattithiah, his sons and his brothers, twelve; ²²to the fifteenth, to Jeremoth, his sons and his brothers, twelve; ²³to the sixteenth, to Hananiah, his sons and his brothers, twelve; ²⁴to the seventeenth, to Joshbekashah, his sons and his brothers, twelve; ²⁵to the eighteenth, to Hanani, his sons and his brothers, twelve; ²⁶to the nineteenth, to Mallothi, his sons and his brothers, twelve; ²⁷to the twentieth, to Eliathah, his sons and his brothers, twelve; ²⁸to the twenty-first, to Hothir, his sons and his brothers, twelve; ²⁹to the twenty-second, to Giddalti, his sons and his brothers, twelve; ³⁰to the twenty-third, to Mahazioth, his sons and his brothers, twelve; ³¹to the twenty-fourth, to Romamti-ezer, his sons and his brothers, twelve.

Divisions of the Gatekeepers

26 As for the divisions of the gatekeepers: of the Korahites, Meshelemiah the son of Kore, of the sons of Asaph. ²And Meshelemiah had sons: Zechariah the firstborn, Jediael the second, Zebadiah the third, Jathniel the fourth, ³Elam the fifth, Jehohanan the sixth, Eliehoenai the seventh. ⁴And Obed-edom had sons: Shemaiah the firstborn, Jehozabad the second, Joah the third, Sachar the fourth, Nethanel the fifth, ⁵Ammiel the sixth, Issachar the seventh, Peullethai the eighth, for God blessed him. ⁶Also to his son Shemaiah were sons born who were rulers in their fathers' houses, for they were men of great ability. ⁷The sons of Shemaiah: Othni, Rephael, Obed and Elzabad, whose brothers were able men, Elihu and Semachiah. ⁸All these were of the sons of Obed-edom with their sons and brothers, able men qualified for the service; sixty-two of Obed-edom. ⁹And Meshelemiah had sons and brothers, able men, eighteen. ¹⁰And Hosah, of the sons of Merari, had sons: Shimri the chief (for though he was not the firstborn, his father made him chief), ¹¹Hilkiah the second, Tebaliah the third, Zechariah the fourth: all the sons and brothers of Hosah were thirteen.

¹²These divisions of the gatekeepers, corresponding to their chief men, had duties, just as their brothers did, ministering in the house of the Lord. ¹³And they cast lots by fathers' houses, small and great alike, for their gates. ¹⁴The lot for the east fell to Shelemiah. They cast lots also for his son Zechariah, a shrewd counselor, and his lot came out for the north. ¹⁵Obed-edom's came out for the south, and to his sons was allotted the gatehouse. ¹⁶For Shuppim and Hosah it came out for the west, at the gate of Shallecheth on the road that goes up. Watch corresponded to watch. ¹⁷On the east there were six each day, on the

north four each day, on the south four each day, as well as two and two at the gatehouse. ¹⁸ And for the colonnade on the west there were four at the road and two at the colonnade. ¹⁹ These were the divisions of the gatekeepers among the Korahites and the sons of Merari.

Treasurers and Other Officials

²⁰ And of the Levites, Ahijah had charge of the treasuries of the house of God and the treasuries of the dedicated gifts. ²¹ The sons of Ladan, the sons of the Gershonites belonging to Ladan, the heads of the fathers' houses belonging to Ladan the Gershonite: Jehieli. ²² The sons of Jehieli, Zetham, and Joel his brother, were in charge of the treasuries of the house of the LORD. ²³ Of the Amramites, the Izharites, the Hebronites, and the Uzzielites— ²⁴ and Shebuel the son of Gershom, son of Moses, was chief officer in charge of the treasuries. ²⁵ His brothers: from Eliezer were his son Rehabiah, and his son Jeshaiah, and his son Joram, and his son Zichri, and his son Shelomoth. ²⁶ This Shelomoth and his brothers were in charge of all the treasuries of the dedicated gifts that David the king and the heads of the fathers' houses and the officers of the thousands and the hundreds and the commanders of the army had dedicated. ²⁷ From spoil won in battles they dedicated gifts for the maintenance of the house of the LORD. ²⁸ Also all that Samuel the seer and Saul the son of Kish and Abner the son of Ner and Joab the son of Zeruiah had dedicated—all dedicated gifts were in the care of Shelomoth and his brothers.

²⁹ Of the Izharites, Chenaniah and his sons were appointed to external duties for Israel, as officers and judges. ³⁰ Of the

Hebronites, Hashabiah and his brothers, 1,700 men of ability, had the oversight of Israel westward of the Jordan for all the work of the LORD and for the service of the king. ³¹ Of the Hebronites, Jerijah was chief of the Hebronites of whatever genealogy or fathers' houses. (In the fortieth year of David's reign search was made and men of great ability among them were found at Jazer in Gilead.) ³² King David appointed him and his brothers, 2,700 men of ability, heads of fathers' houses, to have the oversight of the Reubenites, the Gadites and the half-tribe of the Manassites for everything pertaining to God and for the affairs of the king.

Military Divisions

27 This is the number of the people of Israel, the heads of fathers' houses, the commanders of thousands and hundreds, and their officers who served the king in all matters concerning the divisions that came and went, month after month throughout the year, each division numbering 24,000:

² Jashobeam the son of Zabdiel was in charge of the first division in the first month; in his division were 24,000. ³ He was a descendant of Perez and was chief of all the commanders. He served for the first month. ⁴ Dodai the Ahohite was in charge of the division of the second month; in his division were 24,000. ⁵ The third commander, for the third month, was Benaiah, the son of Jehoiada the chief priest; in his division were 24,000. ⁶ This is the Benaiah who was a mighty man of the thirty and in command of the thirty; Ammizabad his son was in charge of his division. ⁷ Asahel the brother of Joab was fourth, for the fourth month, and his son Zebadiah after him; in his division were 24,000. ⁸ The fifth commander, for the fifth month, was Shamhuth the Izrahite; in his division were

24,000. ⁹ Sixth, for the sixth month, was Ira, the son of Ikkesh the Tekoite; in his division were 24,000. ¹⁰ Seventh, for the seventh month, was Helez the Pelonite, of the sons of Ephraim; in his division were 24,000. ¹¹ Eighth, for the eighth month, was Sibbecai the Hushathite, of the Zerahites; in his division were 24,000. ¹² Ninth, for the ninth month, was Abiezer of Anathoth, a Benjaminite; in his division were 24,000. ¹³ Tenth, for the tenth month, was Maharai of Netophah, of the Zerahites; in his division were 24,000. ¹⁴ Eleventh, for the eleventh month, was Benaiah of Pirathon, of the sons of Ephraim; in his division were 24,000. ¹⁵ Twelfth, for the twelfth month, was Heldai the Netophathite, of Othniel; in his division were 24,000.

Leaders of Tribes

¹⁶ Over the tribes of Israel, for the Reubenites, Eliezer the son of Zichri was chief officer; for the Simeonites, Shephatiah the son of Maacah; ¹⁷ for Levi, Hashabiah the son of Kemuel; for Aaron, Zadok; ¹⁸ for Judah, Elihu, one of David's brothers; for Issachar, Omri the son of Michael; ¹⁹ for Zebulun, Ishmaiah the son of Obadiah; for Naphtali, Jeremoth the son of Azriel; ²⁰ for the Ephraimites, Hoshea the son of Azaziah; for the half-tribe of Manasseh, Joel the son of Pedaiah; ²¹ for the half-tribe of Manasseh in Gilead, Iddo the son of Zechariah; for Benjamin, Jaasiel the son of Abner; ²² for Dan, Azarel the son of Jeroham. These were the leaders of the tribes of Israel. ²³ David did not count those below twenty years of age, for the LORD had promised to make Israel as many as the stars of heaven. ²⁴ Joab the son of Zeruiah began to count, but did not finish. Yet wrath came upon Israel for this, and the number was not entered in the chronicles of King David.

²⁵ Over the king's treasuries was Azmaveth the son of Adiel; and over the treasuries in the country, in the cities, in the villages, and in the towers, was Jonathan the son of Uzziah; ²⁶ and over those who did the work of the field for tilling the soil was Ezri the son of Chelub; ²⁷ and over the vineyards was Shimei the Ramathite; and over the produce of the vineyards for the wine cellars was Zabdi the Shiphmite. ²⁸ Over the olive and sycamore trees in the Shephelah was Baal-hanan the Gederite; and over the stores of oil was Joash. ²⁹ Over the herds that pastured in Sharon was Shitrai the Sharonite; over the herds in the valleys was Shaphat the son of Adlai. ³⁰ Over the camels was Obil the Ishmaelite; and over the donkeys was Jehdeiah the Meronothite. Over the flocks was Jaziz the Hagrite. ³¹ All these were stewards of King David's property.

³² Jonathan, David's uncle, was a counselor, being a man of understanding and a scribe. He and Jehiel the son of Hachmoni attended the king's sons. ³³ Ahithophel was the king's counselor, and Hushai the Archite was the king's friend. ³⁴ Ahithophel was succeeded by Jehoiada the son of Benaiah, and Abiathar. Joab was commander of the king's army.

David's Charge to Israel

28 David assembled at Jerusalem all the officials of Israel, the officials of the tribes, the officers of the divisions that served the king, the commanders of thousands, the commanders of hundreds, the stewards of all the property and livestock of the king and his sons, together with the palace officials, the mighty men and all the seasoned warriors. ² Then King David rose to his feet and said: "Hear me, my brothers and my people. I had it in my heart to build a house of rest for the

ark of the covenant of the LORD and for the footstool of our God, and I made preparations for building. ³ But God said to me, 'You may not build a house for my name, for you are a man of war and have shed blood.' ⁴ Yet the LORD God of Israel chose me from all my father's house to be king over Israel forever. For he chose Judah as leader, and in the house of Judah my father's house, and among my father's sons he took pleasure in me to make me king over all Israel. ⁵ And of all my sons (for the LORD has given me many sons) he has chosen Solomon my son to sit on the throne of the kingdom of the LORD over Israel. ⁶ He said to me, 'It is Solomon your son who shall build my house and my courts, for I have chosen him to be my son, and I will be his father. ⁷ I will establish his kingdom forever if he continues strong in keeping my commandments and my rules, as he is today.' ⁸ Now therefore in the sight of all Israel, the assembly of the LORD, and in the hearing of our God, observe and seek out all the commandments of the LORD your God, that you may possess this good land and leave it for an inheritance to your children after you forever.

David's Charge to Solomon

⁹ "And you, Solomon my son, know the God of your father and serve him with a whole heart and with a willing mind, for the LORD searches all hearts and understands every plan and thought. If you seek him, he will be found by you, but if you forsake him, he will cast you off forever. ¹⁰ Be careful now, for the LORD has chosen you to build a house for the sanctuary; be strong and do it."

¹¹ Then David gave Solomon his son the plan of the vestibule of the temple, and of its houses, its treasuries, its upper rooms,

and its inner chambers, and of the room for the mercy seat; ¹²and the plan of all that he had in mind for the courts of the house of the LORD, all the surrounding chambers, the treasuries of the house of God, and the treasuries for dedicated gifts; ¹³for the divisions of the priests and of the Levites, and all the work of the service in the house of the LORD; for all the vessels for the service in the house of the LORD, ¹⁴the weight of gold for all golden vessels for each service, the weight of silver vessels for each service, ¹⁵the weight of the golden lampstands and their lamps, the weight of gold for each lampstand and its lamps, the weight of silver for a lampstand and its lamps, according to the use of each lampstand in the service, ¹⁶the weight of gold for each table for the showbread, the silver for the silver tables, ¹⁷and pure gold for the forks, the basins and the cups; for the golden bowls and the weight of each; for the silver bowls and the weight of each; ¹⁸for the altar of incense made of refined gold, and its weight; also his plan for the golden chariot of the cherubim that spread their wings and covered the ark of the covenant of the LORD. ¹⁹"All this he made clear to me in writing from the hand of the LORD, all the work to be done according to the plan."

²⁰Then David said to Solomon his son, "Be strong and courageous and do it. Do not be afraid and do not be dismayed, for the LORD God, even my God, is with you. He will not leave you or forsake you, until all the work for the service of the house of the LORD is finished. ²¹And behold the divisions of the priests and the Levites for all the service of the house of God; and with you in all the work will be every willing man who has skill for any kind of service; also the officers and all the people will be wholly at your command."

Offerings for the Temple

29 And David the king said to all the assembly, "Solomon my son, whom alone God has chosen, is young and inexperienced, and the work is great, for the palace will not be for man but for the LORD God. ²So I have provided for the house of my God, so far as I was able, the gold for the things of gold, the silver for the things of silver, and the bronze for the things of bronze, the iron for the things of iron, and wood for the things of wood, besides great quantities of onyx and stones for setting, antimony, colored stones, all sorts of precious stones and marble. ³Moreover, in addition to all that I have provided for the holy house, I have a treasure of my own of gold and silver, and because of my devotion to the house of my God I give it to the house of my God: ⁴3,000 talents of gold, of the gold of Ophir, and 7,000 talents of refined silver, for overlaying the walls of the house, ⁵and for all the work to be done by craftsmen, gold for the things of gold and silver for the things of silver. Who then will offer willingly, consecrating himself today to the LORD?"

⁶Then the leaders of fathers' houses made their freewill offerings, as did also the leaders of the tribes, the commanders of thousands and of hundreds, and the officers over the king's work. ⁷They gave for the service of the house of God 5,000 talents and 10,000 darics of gold, 10,000 talents of silver, 18,000 talents of bronze and 100,000 talents of iron. ⁸And whoever had precious stones gave them to the treasury of the house of the LORD, in the care of Jehiel the Gershonite. ⁹Then the people rejoiced because they had given willingly, for with a whole heart they had offered freely to the LORD. David the king also rejoiced greatly.

David Prays in the Assembly

¹⁰ Therefore David blessed the LORD in the presence of all the assembly. And David said: "Blessed are you, O LORD, the God of Israel our father, forever and ever. ¹¹ Yours, O LORD, is the greatness and the power and the glory and the victory and the majesty, for all that is in the heavens and in the earth is yours. Yours is the kingdom, O LORD, and you are exalted as head above all. ¹² Both riches and honor come from you, and you rule over all. In your hand are power and might, and in your hand it is to make great and to give strength to all. ¹³ And now we thank you, our God, and praise your glorious name.

¹⁴ "But who am I, and what is my people, that we should be able thus to offer willingly? For all things come from you, and of your own have we given you. ¹⁵ For we are strangers before you and sojourners, as all our fathers were. Our days on the earth are like a shadow, and there is no abiding. ¹⁶ O LORD our God, all this abundance that we have provided for building you a house for your holy name comes from your hand and is all your own. ¹⁷ I know, my God, that you test the heart and have pleasure in uprightness. In the uprightness of my heart I have freely offered all these things, and now I have seen your people, who are present here, offering freely and joyously to you. ¹⁸ O LORD, the God of Abraham, Isaac, and Israel, our fathers, keep forever such purposes and thoughts in the hearts of your people, and direct their hearts toward you. ¹⁹ Grant to Solomon my son a whole heart that he may keep your commandments, your testimonies, and your statutes, performing all, and that he may build the palace for which I have made provision."

²⁰ Then David said to all the assembly, "Bless the LORD your God." And all the assembly blessed the LORD, the God of their

fathers, and bowed their heads and paid homage to the LORD and to the king. [21] And they offered sacrifices to the LORD, and on the next day offered burnt offerings to the LORD, 1,000 bulls, 1,000 rams, and 1,000 lambs, with their drink offerings, and sacrifices in abundance for all Israel. [22] And they ate and drank before the LORD on that day with great gladness.

Solomon Anointed King

And they made Solomon the son of David king the second time, and they anointed him as prince for the LORD, and Zadok as priest.

[23] Then Solomon sat on the throne of the LORD as king in place of David his father. And he prospered, and all Israel obeyed him. [24] All the leaders and the mighty men, and also all the sons of King David, pledged their allegiance to King Solomon. [25] And the LORD made Solomon very great in the sight of all Israel and bestowed on him such royal majesty as had not been on any king before him in Israel.

The Death of David

[26] Thus David the son of Jesse reigned over all Israel. [27] The time that he reigned over Israel was forty years. He reigned seven years in Hebron and thirty-three years in Jerusalem. [28] Then he died at a good age, full of days, riches, and honor. And Solomon his son reigned in his place. [29] Now the acts of King David, from first to last, are written in the Chronicles of Samuel the seer, and in the Chronicles of Nathan the prophet, and in the Chronicles of Gad the seer, [30] with accounts of all his rule and his might and of the circumstances that came upon him and upon Israel and upon all the kingdoms of the countries.

2 CHRONICLES

Solomon Worships at Gibeon

1 Solomon the son of David established himself in his kingdom, and the LORD his God was with him and made him exceedingly great.

² Solomon spoke to all Israel, to the commanders of thousands and of hundreds, to the judges, and to all the leaders in all Israel, the heads of fathers' houses. ³ And Solomon, and all the assembly with him, went to the high place that was at Gibeon, for the tent of meeting of God, which Moses the servant of the LORD had made in the wilderness, was there. ⁴ (But David had brought up the ark of God from Kiriath-jearim to the place that David had prepared for it, for he had pitched a tent for it in Jerusalem.) ⁵ Moreover, the bronze altar that Bezalel the son of Uri, son of Hur, had made, was there before the tabernacle of the LORD. And Solomon and the assembly sought it out. ⁶ And Solomon went up there to the bronze altar before the LORD, which was at the tent of meeting, and offered a thousand burnt offerings on it.

Solomon Prays for Wisdom

⁷ In that night God appeared to Solomon, and said to him, "Ask what I shall give you." ⁸ And Solomon said to God, "You have shown great and steadfast love to David my father, and have made me king in his place. ⁹ O LORD God, let your word

to David my father be now fulfilled, for you have made me king over a people as numerous as the dust of the earth. ¹⁰ Give me now wisdom and knowledge to go out and come in before this people, for who can govern this people of yours, which is so great?" ¹¹ God answered Solomon, "Because this was in your heart, and you have not asked for possessions, wealth, honor, or the life of those who hate you, and have not even asked for long life, but have asked for wisdom and knowledge for yourself that you may govern my people over whom I have made you king, ¹² wisdom and knowledge are granted to you. I will also give you riches, possessions, and honor, such as none of the kings had who were before you, and none after you shall have the like." ¹³ So Solomon came from the high place at Gibeon, from before the tent of meeting, to Jerusalem. And he reigned over Israel.

Solomon Given Wealth

¹⁴ Solomon gathered together chariots and horsemen. He had 1,400 chariots and 12,000 horsemen, whom he stationed in the chariot cities and with the king in Jerusalem. ¹⁵ And the king made silver and gold as common in Jerusalem as stone, and he made cedar as plentiful as the sycamore of the Shephelah. ¹⁶ And Solomon's import of horses was from Egypt and Kue, and the king's traders would buy them from Kue for a price. ¹⁷ They imported a chariot from Egypt for 600 shekels of silver, and a horse for 150. Likewise through them these were exported to all the kings of the Hittites and the kings of Syria.

Preparing to Build the Temple

2 Now Solomon purposed to build a temple for the name of the LORD, and a royal palace for himself. ² And Solomon

assigned 70,000 men to bear burdens and 80,000 to quarry in the hill country, and 3,600 to oversee them. ³And Solomon sent word to Hiram the king of Tyre: "As you dealt with David my father and sent him cedar to build himself a house to dwell in, so deal with me. ⁴Behold, I am about to build a house for the name of the Lord my God and dedicate it to him for the burning of incense of sweet spices before him, and for the regular arrangement of the showbread, and for burnt offerings morning and evening, on the Sabbaths and the new moons and the appointed feasts of the Lord our God, as ordained forever for Israel. ⁵The house that I am to build will be great, for our God is greater than all gods. ⁶But who is able to build him a house, since heaven, even highest heaven, cannot contain him? Who am I to build a house for him, except as a place to make offerings before him? ⁷So now send me a man skilled to work in gold, silver, bronze, and iron, and in purple, crimson, and blue fabrics, trained also in engraving, to be with the skilled workers who are with me in Judah and Jerusalem, whom David my father provided. ⁸Send me also cedar, cypress, and algum timber from Lebanon, for I know that your servants know how to cut timber in Lebanon. And my servants will be with your servants, ⁹to prepare timber for me in abundance, for the house I am to build will be great and wonderful. ¹⁰I will give for your servants, the woodsmen who cut timber, 20,000 cors of crushed wheat, 20,000 cors of barley, 20,000 baths of wine, and 20,000 baths of oil."

¹¹Then Hiram the king of Tyre answered in a letter that he sent to Solomon, "Because the Lord loves his people, he has made you king over them." ¹²Hiram also said, "Blessed be the Lord God of Israel, who made heaven and earth, who has given

King David a wise son, who has discretion and understanding, who will build a temple for the LORD and a royal palace for himself.

¹³ "Now I have sent a skilled man, who has understanding, Huram-abi, ¹⁴ the son of a woman of the daughters of Dan, and his father was a man of Tyre. He is trained to work in gold, silver, bronze, iron, stone, and wood, and in purple, blue, and crimson fabrics and fine linen, and to do all sorts of engraving and execute any design that may be assigned him, with your craftsmen, the craftsmen of my lord, David your father. ¹⁵ Now therefore the wheat and barley, oil and wine, of which my lord has spoken, let him send to his servants. ¹⁶ And we will cut whatever timber you need from Lebanon and bring it to you in rafts by sea to Joppa, so that you may take it up to Jerusalem."

¹⁷ Then Solomon counted all the resident aliens who were in the land of Israel, after the census of them that David his father had taken, and there were found 153,600. ¹⁸ Seventy thousand of them he assigned to bear burdens, 80,000 to quarry in the hill country, and 3,600 as overseers to make the people work.

Solomon Builds the Temple

3 Then Solomon began to build the house of the LORD in Jerusalem on Mount Moriah, where the LORD had appeared to David his father, at the place that David had appointed, on the threshing floor of Ornan the Jebusite. ² He began to build in the second month of the fourth year of his reign. ³ These are Solomon's measurements for building the house of God: the length, in cubits of the old standard, was sixty cubits, and the breadth twenty cubits. ⁴ The vestibule in front of the nave of the house was twenty cubits long, equal to the width of the house,

and its height was 120 cubits. He overlaid it on the inside with pure gold. ⁵ The nave he lined with cypress and covered it with fine gold and made palms and chains on it. ⁶ He adorned the house with settings of precious stones. The gold was gold of Parvaim. ⁷ So he lined the house with gold—its beams, its thresholds, its walls, and its doors—and he carved cherubim on the walls.

⁸ And he made the Most Holy Place. Its length, corresponding to the breadth of the house, was twenty cubits, and its breadth was twenty cubits. He overlaid it with 600 talents of fine gold. ⁹ The weight of gold for the nails was fifty shekels. And he overlaid the upper chambers with gold.

¹⁰ In the Most Holy Place he made two cherubim of wood and overlaid them with gold. ¹¹ The wings of the cherubim together extended twenty cubits: one wing of the one, of five cubits, touched the wall of the house, and its other wing, of five cubits, touched the wing of the other cherub; ¹² and of this cherub, one wing, of five cubits, touched the wall of the house, and the other wing, also of five cubits, was joined to the wing of the first cherub. ¹³ The wings of these cherubim extended twenty cubits. The cherubim stood on their feet, facing the nave. ¹⁴ And he made the veil of blue and purple and crimson fabrics and fine linen, and he worked cherubim on it.

¹⁵ In front of the house he made two pillars thirty-five cubits high, with a capital of five cubits on the top of each. ¹⁶ He made chains like a necklace and put them on the tops of the pillars, and he made a hundred pomegranates and put them on the chains. ¹⁷ He set up the pillars in front of the temple, one on the south, the other on the north; that on the south he called Jachin, and that on the north Boaz.

The Temple's Furnishings

4 He made an altar of bronze, twenty cubits long and twenty cubits wide and ten cubits high. ²Then he made the sea of cast metal. It was round, ten cubits from brim to brim, and five cubits high, and a line of thirty cubits measured its circumference. ³Under it were figures of gourds, for ten cubits, compassing the sea all around. The gourds were in two rows, cast with it when it was cast. ⁴It stood on twelve oxen, three facing north, three facing west, three facing south, and three facing east. The sea was set on them, and all their rear parts were inward. ⁵Its thickness was a handbreadth. And its brim was made like the brim of a cup, like the flower of a lily. It held 3,000 baths. ⁶He also made ten basins in which to wash, and set five on the south side, and five on the north side. In these they were to rinse off what was used for the burnt offering, and the sea was for the priests to wash in.

⁷And he made ten golden lampstands as prescribed, and set them in the temple, five on the south side and five on the north. ⁸He also made ten tables and placed them in the temple, five on the south side and five on the north. And he made a hundred basins of gold. ⁹He made the court of the priests and the great court and doors for the court and overlaid their doors with bronze. ¹⁰And he set the sea at the southeast corner of the house.

¹¹Hiram also made the pots, the shovels, and the basins. So Hiram finished the work that he did for King Solomon on the house of God: ¹²the two pillars, the bowls, and the two capitals on the top of the pillars; and the two latticeworks to cover the two bowls of the capitals that were on the top of the pillars; ¹³and the 400 pomegranates for the two latticeworks, two rows of pomegranates for each latticework, to cover the two bowls of

the capitals that were on the pillars. ¹⁴ He made the stands also, and the basins on the stands, ¹⁵ and the one sea, and the twelve oxen underneath it. ¹⁶ The pots, the shovels, the forks, and all the equipment for these Huram-abi made of burnished bronze for King Solomon for the house of the LORD. ¹⁷ In the plain of the Jordan the king cast them, in the clay ground between Succoth and Zeredah. ¹⁸ Solomon made all these things in great quantities, for the weight of the bronze was not sought.

¹⁹ So Solomon made all the vessels that were in the house of God: the golden altar, the tables for the bread of the Presence, ²⁰ the lampstands and their lamps of pure gold to burn before the inner sanctuary, as prescribed; ²¹ the flowers, the lamps, and the tongs, of purest gold; ²² the snuffers, basins, dishes for incense, and fire pans, of pure gold, and the sockets of the temple, for the inner doors to the Most Holy Place and for the doors of the nave of the temple were of gold.

5 Thus all the work that Solomon did for the house of the LORD was finished. And Solomon brought in the things that David his father had dedicated, and stored the silver, the gold, and all the vessels in the treasuries of the house of God.

The Ark Brought to the Temple

² Then Solomon assembled the elders of Israel and all the heads of the tribes, the leaders of the fathers' houses of the people of Israel, in Jerusalem, to bring up the ark of the covenant of the LORD out of the city of David, which is Zion. ³ And all the men of Israel assembled before the king at the feast that is in the seventh month. ⁴ And all the elders of Israel came, and the Levites took up the ark. ⁵ And they brought up the ark, the tent of meeting, and all the holy vessels that were in the tent; the Levitical priests

brought them up. ⁶And King Solomon and all the congregation of Israel, who had assembled before him, were before the ark, sacrificing so many sheep and oxen that they could not be counted or numbered. ⁷Then the priests brought the ark of the covenant of the LORD to its place, in the inner sanctuary of the house, in the Most Holy Place, underneath the wings of the cherubim. ⁸The cherubim spread out their wings over the place of the ark, so that the cherubim made a covering above the ark and its poles. ⁹And the poles were so long that the ends of the poles were seen from the Holy Place before the inner sanctuary, but they could not be seen from outside. And they are there to this day. ¹⁰There was nothing in the ark except the two tablets that Moses put there at Horeb, where the LORD made a covenant with the people of Israel, when they came out of Egypt. ¹¹And when the priests came out of the Holy Place (for all the priests who were present had consecrated themselves, without regard to their divisions, ¹²and all the Levitical singers, Asaph, Heman, and Jeduthun, their sons and kinsmen, arrayed in fine linen, with cymbals, harps, and lyres, stood east of the altar with 120 priests who were trumpeters; ¹³and it was the duty of the trumpeters and singers to make themselves heard in unison in praise and thanksgiving to the LORD), and when the song was raised, with trumpets and cymbals and other musical instruments, in praise to the LORD,

> "For he is good,
>   for his steadfast love endures forever,"

the house, the house of the LORD, was filled with a cloud, ¹⁴so that the priests could not stand to minister because of the cloud, for the glory of the LORD filled the house of God.

Solomon Blesses the People

6 Then Solomon said, "The LORD has said that he would dwell in thick darkness. ²But I have built you an exalted house, a place for you to dwell in forever." ³Then the king turned around and blessed all the assembly of Israel, while all the assembly of Israel stood. ⁴And he said, "Blessed be the LORD, the God of Israel, who with his hand has fulfilled what he promised with his mouth to David my father, saying, ⁵'Since the day that I brought my people out of the land of Egypt, I chose no city out of all the tribes of Israel in which to build a house, that my name might be there, and I chose no man as prince over my people Israel; ⁶but I have chosen Jerusalem that my name may be there, and I have chosen David to be over my people Israel.' ⁷Now it was in the heart of David my father to build a house for the name of the LORD, the God of Israel. ⁸But the LORD said to David my father, 'Whereas it was in your heart to build a house for my name, you did well that it was in your heart. ⁹Nevertheless, it is not you who shall build the house, but your son who shall be born to you shall build the house for my name.' ¹⁰Now the LORD has fulfilled his promise that he made. For I have risen in the place of David my father and sit on the throne of Israel, as the LORD promised, and I have built the house for the name of the LORD, the God of Israel. ¹¹And there I have set the ark, in which is the covenant of the LORD that he made with the people of Israel."

Solomon's Prayer of Dedication

¹²Then Solomon stood before the altar of the LORD in the presence of all the assembly of Israel and spread out his hands. ¹³Solomon had made a bronze platform five cubits long, five

cubits wide, and three cubits high, and had set it in the court, and he stood on it. Then he knelt on his knees in the presence of all the assembly of Israel, and spread out his hands toward heaven, ¹⁴ and said, "O LORD, God of Israel, there is no God like you, in heaven or on earth, keeping covenant and showing steadfast love to your servants who walk before you with all their heart, ¹⁵ who have kept with your servant David my father what you declared to him. You spoke with your mouth, and with your hand have fulfilled it this day. ¹⁶ Now therefore, O LORD, God of Israel, keep for your servant David my father what you have promised him, saying, 'You shall not lack a man to sit before me on the throne of Israel, if only your sons pay close attention to their way, to walk in my law as you have walked before me.' ¹⁷ Now therefore, O LORD, God of Israel, let your word be confirmed, which you have spoken to your servant David.

¹⁸ "But will God indeed dwell with man on the earth? Behold, heaven and the highest heaven cannot contain you, how much less this house that I have built! ¹⁹ Yet have regard to the prayer of your servant and to his plea, O LORD my God, listening to the cry and to the prayer that your servant prays before you, ²⁰ that your eyes may be open day and night toward this house, the place where you have promised to set your name, that you may listen to the prayer that your servant offers toward this place. ²¹ And listen to the pleas of your servant and of your people Israel, when they pray toward this place. And listen from heaven your dwelling place, and when you hear, forgive.

²² "If a man sins against his neighbor and is made to take an oath and comes and swears his oath before your altar in this house, ²³ then hear from heaven and act and judge your servants,

repaying the guilty by bringing his conduct on his own head, and vindicating the righteous by rewarding him according to his righteousness.

²⁴ "If your people Israel are defeated before the enemy because they have sinned against you, and they turn again and acknowledge your name and pray and plead with you in this house, ²⁵ then hear from heaven and forgive the sin of your people Israel and bring them again to the land that you gave to them and to their fathers.

²⁶ "When heaven is shut up and there is no rain because they have sinned against you, if they pray toward this place and acknowledge your name and turn from their sin, when you afflict them, ²⁷ then hear in heaven and forgive the sin of your servants, your people Israel, when you teach them the good way in which they should walk, and grant rain upon your land, which you have given to your people as an inheritance.

²⁸ "If there is famine in the land, if there is pestilence or blight or mildew or locust or caterpillar, if their enemies besiege them in the land at their gates, whatever plague, whatever sickness there is, ²⁹ whatever prayer, whatever plea is made by any man or by all your people Israel, each knowing his own affliction and his own sorrow and stretching out his hands toward this house, ³⁰ then hear from heaven your dwelling place and forgive and render to each whose heart you know, according to all his ways, for you, you only, know the hearts of the children of mankind, ³¹ that they may fear you and walk in your ways all the days that they live in the land that you gave to our fathers.

³² "Likewise, when a foreigner, who is not of your people Israel, comes from a far country for the sake of your great name and your mighty hand and your outstretched arm, when he

comes and prays toward this house, [33] hear from heaven your dwelling place and do according to all for which the foreigner calls to you, in order that all the peoples of the earth may know your name and fear you, as do your people Israel, and that they may know that this house that I have built is called by your name.

[34] "If your people go out to battle against their enemies, by whatever way you shall send them, and they pray to you toward this city that you have chosen and the house that I have built for your name, [35] then hear from heaven their prayer and their plea, and maintain their cause.

[36] "If they sin against you—for there is no one who does not sin—and you are angry with them and give them to an enemy, so that they are carried away captive to a land far or near, [37] yet if they turn their heart in the land to which they have been carried captive, and repent and plead with you in the land of their captivity, saying, 'We have sinned and have acted perversely and wickedly,' [38] if they repent with all their heart and with all their soul in the land of their captivity to which they were carried captive, and pray toward their land, which you gave to their fathers, the city that you have chosen and the house that I have built for your name, [39] then hear from heaven your dwelling place their prayer and their pleas, and maintain their cause and forgive your people who have sinned against you. [40] Now, O my God, let your eyes be open and your ears attentive to the prayer of this place.

[41]   "And now arise, O LORD God, and go to your resting
          place,
       you and the ark of your might.

> Let your priests, O L ORD God, be clothed with
>   salvation,
>   and let your saints rejoice in your goodness.
> 42 O L ORD God, do not turn away the face of your
>   anointed one!
>   Remember your steadfast love for David your
>   servant."

Fire from Heaven

7 As soon as Solomon finished his prayer, fire came down from heaven and consumed the burnt offering and the sacrifices, and the glory of the L ORD filled the temple. ²And the priests could not enter the house of the L ORD, because the glory of the L ORD filled the L ORD's house. ³When all the people of Israel saw the fire come down and the glory of the L ORD on the temple, they bowed down with their faces to the ground on the pavement and worshiped and gave thanks to the L ORD, saying, "For he is good, for his steadfast love endures forever."

The Dedication of the Temple

⁴Then the king and all the people offered sacrifice before the L ORD. ⁵King Solomon offered as a sacrifice 22,000 oxen and 120,000 sheep. So the king and all the people dedicated the house of God. ⁶The priests stood at their posts; the Levites also, with the instruments for music to the L ORD that King David had made for giving thanks to the L ORD—for his steadfast love endures forever—whenever David offered praises by their ministry; opposite them the priests sounded trumpets, and all Israel stood.

⁷And Solomon consecrated the middle of the court that was before the house of the LORD, for there he offered the burnt offering and the fat of the peace offerings, because the bronze altar Solomon had made could not hold the burnt offering and the grain offering and the fat.

⁸At that time Solomon held the feast for seven days, and all Israel with him, a very great assembly, from Lebo-hamath to the Brook of Egypt. ⁹And on the eighth day they held a solemn assembly, for they had kept the dedication of the altar seven days and the feast seven days. ¹⁰On the twenty-third day of the seventh month he sent the people away to their homes, joyful and glad of heart for the prosperity that the LORD had granted to David and to Solomon and to Israel his people.

If My People Pray

¹¹Thus Solomon finished the house of the LORD and the king's house. All that Solomon had planned to do in the house of the LORD and in his own house he successfully accomplished. ¹²Then the LORD appeared to Solomon in the night and said to him: "I have heard your prayer and have chosen this place for myself as a house of sacrifice. ¹³When I shut up the heavens so that there is no rain, or command the locust to devour the land, or send pestilence among my people, ¹⁴if my people who are called by my name humble themselves, and pray and seek my face and turn from their wicked ways, then I will hear from heaven and will forgive their sin and heal their land. ¹⁵Now my eyes will be open and my ears attentive to the prayer that is made in this place. ¹⁶For now I have chosen and consecrated this house that my name may be there forever. My eyes and my heart will be there for all time. ¹⁷And as for you, if you will walk

before me as David your father walked, doing according to all that I have commanded you and keeping my statutes and my rules, [18] then I will establish your royal throne, as I covenanted with David your father, saying, 'You shall not lack a man to rule Israel.'

[19] "But if you turn aside and forsake my statutes and my commandments that I have set before you, and go and serve other gods and worship them, [20] then I will pluck you up from my land that I have given you, and this house that I have consecrated for my name, I will cast out of my sight, and I will make it a proverb and a byword among all peoples. [21] And at this house, which was exalted, everyone passing by will be astonished and say, 'Why has the LORD done thus to this land and to this house?' [22] Then they will say, 'Because they abandoned the LORD, the God of their fathers who brought them out of the land of Egypt, and laid hold on other gods and worshiped them and served them. Therefore he has brought all this disaster on them.'"

Solomon's Accomplishments

8 At the end of twenty years, in which Solomon had built the house of the LORD and his own house, [2] Solomon rebuilt the cities that Hiram had given to him, and settled the people of Israel in them.

[3] And Solomon went to Hamath-zobah and took it. [4] He built Tadmor in the wilderness and all the store cities that he built in Hamath. [5] He also built Upper Beth-horon and Lower Beth-horon, fortified cities with walls, gates, and bars, [6] and Baalath, and all the store cities that Solomon had and all the cities for his chariots and the cities for his horsemen, and whatever Solomon desired to build in Jerusalem, in Lebanon, and in

all the land of his dominion. ⁷All the people who were left of the Hittites, the Amorites, the Perizzites, the Hivites, and the Jebusites, who were not of Israel, ⁸from their descendants who were left after them in the land, whom the people of Israel had not destroyed—these Solomon drafted as forced labor, and so they are to this day. ⁹But of the people of Israel Solomon made no slaves for his work; they were soldiers, and his officers, the commanders of his chariots, and his horsemen. ¹⁰And these were the chief officers of King Solomon, 250, who exercised authority over the people.

¹¹Solomon brought Pharaoh's daughter up from the city of David to the house that he had built for her, for he said, "My wife shall not live in the house of David king of Israel, for the places to which the ark of the LORD has come are holy."

¹²Then Solomon offered up burnt offerings to the LORD on the altar of the LORD that he had built before the vestibule, ¹³as the duty of each day required, offering according to the commandment of Moses for the Sabbaths, the new moons, and the three annual feasts—the Feast of Unleavened Bread, the Feast of Weeks, and the Feast of Booths. ¹⁴According to the ruling of David his father, he appointed the divisions of the priests for their service, and the Levites for their offices of praise and ministry before the priests as the duty of each day required, and the gatekeepers in their divisions at each gate, for so David the man of God had commanded. ¹⁵And they did not turn aside from what the king had commanded the priests and Levites concerning any matter and concerning the treasuries.

¹⁶Thus was accomplished all the work of Solomon from the day the foundation of the house of the LORD was laid until it was finished. So the house of the LORD was completed.

¹⁷Then Solomon went to Ezion-geber and Eloth on the shore of the sea, in the land of Edom. ¹⁸And Hiram sent to him by the hand of his servants ships and servants familiar with the sea, and they went to Ophir together with the servants of Solomon and brought from there 450 talents of gold and brought it to King Solomon.

The Queen of Sheba

9 Now when the queen of Sheba heard of the fame of Solomon, she came to Jerusalem to test him with hard questions, having a very great retinue and camels bearing spices and very much gold and precious stones. And when she came to Solomon, she told him all that was on her mind. ²And Solomon answered all her questions. There was nothing hidden from Solomon that he could not explain to her. ³And when the queen of Sheba had seen the wisdom of Solomon, the house that he had built, ⁴the food of his table, the seating of his officials, and the attendance of his servants, and their clothing, his cupbearers, and their clothing, and his burnt offerings that he offered at the house of the LORD, there was no more breath in her.

⁵And she said to the king, "The report was true that I heard in my own land of your words and of your wisdom, ⁶but I did not believe the reports until I came and my own eyes had seen it. And behold, half the greatness of your wisdom was not told me; you surpass the report that I heard. ⁷Happy are your wives! Happy are these your servants, who continually stand before you and hear your wisdom! ⁸Blessed be the LORD your God, who has delighted in you and set you on his throne as king for the LORD your God! Because your God loved Israel and would establish them forever, he has made you king over them, that

you may execute justice and righteousness." [9] Then she gave the king 120 talents of gold, and a very great quantity of spices, and precious stones. There were no spices such as those that the queen of Sheba gave to King Solomon.

[10] Moreover, the servants of Hiram and the servants of Solomon, who brought gold from Ophir, brought algum wood and precious stones. [11] And the king made from the algum wood supports for the house of the LORD and for the king's house, lyres also and harps for the singers. There never was seen the like of them before in the land of Judah.

[12] And King Solomon gave to the queen of Sheba all that she desired, whatever she asked besides what she had brought to the king. So she turned and went back to her own land with her servants.

Solomon's Wealth

[13] Now the weight of gold that came to Solomon in one year was 666 talents of gold, [14] besides that which the explorers and merchants brought. And all the kings of Arabia and the governors of the land brought gold and silver to Solomon. [15] King Solomon made 200 large shields of beaten gold; 600 shekels of beaten gold went into each shield. [16] And he made 300 shields of beaten gold; 300 shekels of gold went into each shield; and the king put them in the House of the Forest of Lebanon. [17] The king also made a great ivory throne and overlaid it with pure gold. [18] The throne had six steps and a footstool of gold, which were attached to the throne, and on each side of the seat were armrests and two lions standing beside the armrests, [19] while twelve lions stood there, one on each end of a step on the six steps. Nothing like it was ever made for

any kingdom. [20] All King Solomon's drinking vessels were of gold, and all the vessels of the House of the Forest of Lebanon were of pure gold. Silver was not considered as anything in the days of Solomon. [21] For the king's ships went to Tarshish with the servants of Hiram. Once every three years the ships of Tarshish used to come bringing gold, silver, ivory, apes, and peacocks.

[22] Thus King Solomon excelled all the kings of the earth in riches and in wisdom. [23] And all the kings of the earth sought the presence of Solomon to hear his wisdom, which God had put into his mind. [24] Every one of them brought his present, articles of silver and of gold, garments, myrrh, spices, horses, and mules, so much year by year. [25] And Solomon had 4,000 stalls for horses and chariots, and 12,000 horsemen, whom he stationed in the chariot cities and with the king in Jerusalem. [26] And he ruled over all the kings from the Euphrates to the land of the Philistines and to the border of Egypt. [27] And the king made silver as common in Jerusalem as stone, and he made cedar as plentiful as the sycamore of the Shephelah. [28] And horses were imported for Solomon from Egypt and from all lands.

Solomon's Death

[29] Now the rest of the acts of Solomon, from first to last, are they not written in the history of Nathan the prophet, and in the prophecy of Ahijah the Shilonite, and in the visions of Iddo the seer concerning Jeroboam the son of Nebat? [30] Solomon reigned in Jerusalem over all Israel forty years. [31] And Solomon slept with his fathers and was buried in the city of David his father, and Rehoboam his son reigned in his place.

The Revolt Against Rehoboam

10 Rehoboam went to Shechem, for all Israel had come to Shechem to make him king. ²And as soon as Jeroboam the son of Nebat heard of it (for he was in Egypt, where he had fled from King Solomon), then Jeroboam returned from Egypt. ³And they sent and called him. And Jeroboam and all Israel came and said to Rehoboam, ⁴"Your father made our yoke heavy. Now therefore lighten the hard service of your father and his heavy yoke on us, and we will serve you." ⁵He said to them, "Come to me again in three days." So the people went away.

⁶Then King Rehoboam took counsel with the old men, who had stood before Solomon his father while he was yet alive, saying, "How do you advise me to answer this people?" ⁷And they said to him, "If you will be good to this people and please them and speak good words to them, then they will be your servants forever." ⁸But he abandoned the counsel that the old men gave him, and took counsel with the young men who had grown up with him and stood before him. ⁹And he said to them, "What do you advise that we answer this people who have said to me, 'Lighten the yoke that your father put on us'?" ¹⁰And the young men who had grown up with him said to him, "Thus shall you speak to the people who said to you, 'Your father made our yoke heavy, but you lighten it for us'; thus shall you say to them, 'My little finger is thicker than my father's thighs. ¹¹And now, whereas my father laid on you a heavy yoke, I will add to your yoke. My father disciplined you with whips, but I will discipline you with scorpions.'"

¹²So Jeroboam and all the people came to Rehoboam the third day, as the king said, "Come to me again the third day."

¹³ And the king answered them harshly; and forsaking the counsel of the old men, ¹⁴ King Rehoboam spoke to them according to the counsel of the young men, saying, "My father made your yoke heavy, but I will add to it. My father disciplined you with whips, but I will discipline you with scorpions." ¹⁵ So the king did not listen to the people, for it was a turn of affairs brought about by God that the LORD might fulfill his word, which he spoke by Ahijah the Shilonite to Jeroboam the son of Nebat.

¹⁶ And when all Israel saw that the king did not listen to them, the people answered the king, "What portion have we in David? We have no inheritance in the son of Jesse. Each of you to your tents, O Israel! Look now to your own house, David." So all Israel went to their tents. ¹⁷ But Rehoboam reigned over the people of Israel who lived in the cities of Judah. ¹⁸ Then King Rehoboam sent Hadoram, who was taskmaster over the forced labor, and the people of Israel stoned him to death with stones. And King Rehoboam quickly mounted his chariot to flee to Jerusalem. ¹⁹ So Israel has been in rebellion against the house of David to this day.

Rehoboam Secures His Kingdom

11 When Rehoboam came to Jerusalem, he assembled the house of Judah and Benjamin, 180,000 chosen warriors, to fight against Israel, to restore the kingdom to Rehoboam. ² But the word of the LORD came to Shemaiah the man of God: ³ "Say to Rehoboam the son of Solomon, king of Judah, and to all Israel in Judah and Benjamin, ⁴ 'Thus says the LORD, You shall not go up or fight against your relatives. Return every man to his home, for this thing is from me.'" So they listened

to the word of the LORD and returned and did not go against Jeroboam.

⁵ Rehoboam lived in Jerusalem, and he built cities for defense in Judah. ⁶ He built Bethlehem, Etam, Tekoa, ⁷ Beth-zur, Soco, Adullam, ⁸ Gath, Mareshah, Ziph, ⁹ Adoraim, Lachish, Azekah, ¹⁰ Zorah, Aijalon, and Hebron, fortified cities that are in Judah and in Benjamin. ¹¹ He made the fortresses strong, and put commanders in them, and stores of food, oil, and wine. ¹² And he put shields and spears in all the cities and made them very strong. So he held Judah and Benjamin.

Priests and Levites Come to Jerusalem

¹³ And the priests and the Levites who were in all Israel presented themselves to him from all places where they lived. ¹⁴ For the Levites left their common lands and their holdings and came to Judah and Jerusalem, because Jeroboam and his sons cast them out from serving as priests of the LORD, ¹⁵ and he appointed his own priests for the high places and for the goat idols and for the calves that he had made. ¹⁶ And those who had set their hearts to seek the LORD God of Israel came after them from all the tribes of Israel to Jerusalem to sacrifice to the LORD, the God of their fathers. ¹⁷ They strengthened the kingdom of Judah, and for three years they made Rehoboam the son of Solomon secure, for they walked for three years in the way of David and Solomon.

Rehoboam's Family

¹⁸ Rehoboam took as wife Mahalath the daughter of Jerimoth the son of David, and of Abihail the daughter of Eliab the son of Jesse, ¹⁹ and she bore him sons, Jeush, Shemariah, and

Zaham. ²⁰ After her he took Maacah the daughter of Absalom, who bore him Abijah, Attai, Ziza, and Shelomith. ²¹ Rehoboam loved Maacah the daughter of Absalom above all his wives and concubines (he took eighteen wives and sixty concubines, and fathered twenty-eight sons and sixty daughters). ²² And Rehoboam appointed Abijah the son of Maacah as chief prince among his brothers, for he intended to make him king. ²³ And he dealt wisely and distributed some of his sons through all the districts of Judah and Benjamin, in all the fortified cities, and he gave them abundant provisions and procured wives for them.

Egypt Plunders Jerusalem

12 When the rule of Rehoboam was established and he was strong, he abandoned the law of the LORD, and all Israel with him. ² In the fifth year of King Rehoboam, because they had been unfaithful to the LORD, Shishak king of Egypt came up against Jerusalem ³ with 1,200 chariots and 60,000 horsemen. And the people were without number who came with him from Egypt—Libyans, Sukkiim, and Ethiopians. ⁴ And he took the fortified cities of Judah and came as far as Jerusalem. ⁵ Then Shemaiah the prophet came to Rehoboam and to the princes of Judah, who had gathered at Jerusalem because of Shishak, and said to them, "Thus says the LORD, 'You abandoned me, so I have abandoned you to the hand of Shishak.'" ⁶ Then the princes of Israel and the king humbled themselves and said, "The LORD is righteous." ⁷ When the LORD saw that they humbled themselves, the word of the LORD came to Shemaiah: "They have humbled themselves. I will not destroy them, but I will grant them some deliverance, and my wrath shall not be poured out on Jerusalem by the hand of Shishak. ⁸ Nevertheless,

they shall be servants to him, that they may know my service and the service of the kingdoms of the countries."

⁹ So Shishak king of Egypt came up against Jerusalem. He took away the treasures of the house of the LORD and the treasures of the king's house. He took away everything. He also took away the shields of gold that Solomon had made, ¹⁰ and King Rehoboam made in their place shields of bronze and committed them to the hands of the officers of the guard, who kept the door of the king's house. ¹¹ And as often as the king went into the house of the LORD, the guard came and carried them and brought them back to the guardroom. ¹² And when he humbled himself the wrath of the LORD turned from him, so as not to make a complete destruction. Moreover, conditions were good in Judah.

¹³ So King Rehoboam grew strong in Jerusalem and reigned. Rehoboam was forty-one years old when he began to reign, and he reigned seventeen years in Jerusalem, the city that the LORD had chosen out of all the tribes of Israel to put his name there. His mother's name was Naamah the Ammonite. ¹⁴ And he did evil, for he did not set his heart to seek the LORD.

¹⁵ Now the acts of Rehoboam, from first to last, are they not written in the chronicles of Shemaiah the prophet and of Iddo the seer? There were continual wars between Rehoboam and Jeroboam. ¹⁶ And Rehoboam slept with his fathers and was buried in the city of David, and Abijah his son reigned in his place.

Abijah Reigns in Judah

13 In the eighteenth year of King Jeroboam, Abijah began to reign over Judah. ² He reigned for three years in Jerusalem. His mother's name was Micaiah the daughter of Uriel of Gibeah.

Now there was war between Abijah and Jeroboam. ³Abijah went out to battle, having an army of valiant men of war, 400,000 chosen men. And Jeroboam drew up his line of battle against him with 800,000 chosen mighty warriors. ⁴Then Abijah stood up on Mount Zemaraim that is in the hill country of Ephraim and said, "Hear me, O Jeroboam and all Israel! ⁵Ought you not to know that the LORD God of Israel gave the kingship over Israel forever to David and his sons by a covenant of salt? ⁶Yet Jeroboam the son of Nebat, a servant of Solomon the son of David, rose up and rebelled against his lord, ⁷and certain worthless scoundrels gathered about him and defied Rehoboam the son of Solomon, when Rehoboam was young and irresolute and could not withstand them.

⁸"And now you think to withstand the kingdom of the LORD in the hand of the sons of David, because you are a great multitude and have with you the golden calves that Jeroboam made you for gods. ⁹Have you not driven out the priests of the LORD, the sons of Aaron, and the Levites, and made priests for yourselves like the peoples of other lands? Whoever comes for ordination with a young bull or seven rams becomes a priest of what are not gods. ¹⁰But as for us, the LORD is our God, and we have not forsaken him. We have priests ministering to the LORD who are sons of Aaron, and Levites for their service. ¹¹They offer to the LORD every morning and every evening burnt offerings and incense of sweet spices, set out the showbread on the table of pure gold, and care for the golden lampstand that its lamps may burn every evening. For we keep the charge of the LORD our God, but you have forsaken him. ¹²Behold, God is with us at our head, and his priests with their battle trumpets to sound the call to battle against you. O sons of Israel, do not

fight against the LORD, the God of your fathers, for you cannot succeed."

¹³ Jeroboam had sent an ambush around to come upon them from behind. Thus his troops were in front of Judah, and the ambush was behind them. ¹⁴ And when Judah looked, behold, the battle was in front of and behind them. And they cried to the LORD, and the priests blew the trumpets. ¹⁵ Then the men of Judah raised the battle shout. And when the men of Judah shouted, God defeated Jeroboam and all Israel before Abijah and Judah. ¹⁶ The men of Israel fled before Judah, and God gave them into their hand. ¹⁷ Abijah and his people struck them with great force, so there fell slain of Israel 500,000 chosen men. ¹⁸ Thus the men of Israel were subdued at that time, and the men of Judah prevailed, because they relied on the LORD, the God of their fathers. ¹⁹ And Abijah pursued Jeroboam and took cities from him, Bethel with its villages and Jeshanah with its villages and Ephron with its villages. ²⁰ Jeroboam did not recover his power in the days of Abijah. And the LORD struck him down, and he died. ²¹ But Abijah grew mighty. And he took fourteen wives and had twenty-two sons and sixteen daughters. ²² The rest of the acts of Abijah, his ways and his sayings, are written in the story of the prophet Iddo.

Asa Reigns in Judah

14 Abijah slept with his fathers, and they buried him in the city of David. And Asa his son reigned in his place. In his days the land had rest for ten years. ² And Asa did what was good and right in the eyes of the LORD his God. ³ He took away the foreign altars and the high places and broke down the pillars and cut down the Asherim ⁴ and commanded Judah to

seek the LORD, the God of their fathers, and to keep the law and the commandment. ⁵He also took out of all the cities of Judah the high places and the incense altars. And the kingdom had rest under him. ⁶He built fortified cities in Judah, for the land had rest. He had no war in those years, for the LORD gave him peace. ⁷And he said to Judah, "Let us build these cities and surround them with walls and towers, gates and bars. The land is still ours, because we have sought the LORD our God. We have sought him, and he has given us peace on every side." So they built and prospered. ⁸And Asa had an army of 300,000 from Judah, armed with large shields and spears, and 280,000 men from Benjamin that carried shields and drew bows. All these were mighty men of valor.

⁹Zerah the Ethiopian came out against them with an army of a million men and 300 chariots, and came as far as Mareshah. ¹⁰And Asa went out to meet him, and they drew up their lines of battle in the Valley of Zephathah at Mareshah. ¹¹And Asa cried to the LORD his God, "O LORD, there is none like you to help, between the mighty and the weak. Help us, O LORD our God, for we rely on you, and in your name we have come against this multitude. O LORD, you are our God; let not man prevail against you." ¹²So the LORD defeated the Ethiopians before Asa and before Judah, and the Ethiopians fled. ¹³Asa and the people who were with him pursued them as far as Gerar, and the Ethiopians fell until none remained alive, for they were broken before the LORD and his army. The men of Judah carried away very much spoil. ¹⁴And they attacked all the cities around Gerar, for the fear of the LORD was upon them. They plundered all the cities, for there was much plunder in them. ¹⁵And they struck down the tents of those who had livestock and carried

away sheep in abundance and camels. Then they returned to Jerusalem.

Asa's Religious Reforms

15 The Spirit of God came upon Azariah the son of Oded, ² and he went out to meet Asa and said to him, "Hear me, Asa, and all Judah and Benjamin: The LORD is with you while you are with him. If you seek him, he will be found by you, but if you forsake him, he will forsake you. ³ For a long time Israel was without the true God, and without a teaching priest and without law, ⁴ but when in their distress they turned to the LORD, the God of Israel, and sought him, he was found by them. ⁵ In those times there was no peace to him who went out or to him who came in, for great disturbances afflicted all the inhabitants of the lands. ⁶ They were broken in pieces. Nation was crushed by nation and city by city, for God troubled them with every sort of distress. ⁷ But you, take courage! Do not let your hands be weak, for your work shall be rewarded."

⁸ As soon as Asa heard these words, the prophecy of Azariah the son of Oded, he took courage and put away the detestable idols from all the land of Judah and Benjamin and from the cities that he had taken in the hill country of Ephraim, and he repaired the altar of the LORD that was in front of the vestibule of the house of the LORD. ⁹ And he gathered all Judah and Benjamin, and those from Ephraim, Manasseh, and Simeon who were residing with them, for great numbers had deserted to him from Israel when they saw that the LORD his God was with him. ¹⁰ They were gathered at Jerusalem in the third month of the fifteenth year of the reign of Asa. ¹¹ They sacrificed to the LORD on that day from the spoil that they had brought 700 oxen

and 7,000 sheep. ¹²And they entered into a covenant to seek the LORD, the God of their fathers, with all their heart and with all their soul, ¹³but that whoever would not seek the LORD, the God of Israel, should be put to death, whether young or old, man or woman. ¹⁴They swore an oath to the LORD with a loud voice and with shouting and with trumpets and with horns. ¹⁵And all Judah rejoiced over the oath, for they had sworn with all their heart and had sought him with their whole desire, and he was found by them, and the LORD gave them rest all around.

¹⁶Even Maacah, his mother, King Asa removed from being queen mother because she had made a detestable image for Asherah. Asa cut down her image, crushed it, and burned it at the brook Kidron. ¹⁷But the high places were not taken out of Israel. Nevertheless, the heart of Asa was wholly true all his days. ¹⁸And he brought into the house of God the sacred gifts of his father and his own sacred gifts, silver, and gold, and vessels. ¹⁹And there was no more war until the thirty-fifth year of the reign of Asa.

Asa's Last Years

16 In the thirty-sixth year of the reign of Asa, Baasha king of Israel went up against Judah and built Ramah, that he might permit no one to go out or come in to Asa king of Judah. ²Then Asa took silver and gold from the treasures of the house of the LORD and the king's house and sent them to Ben-hadad king of Syria, who lived in Damascus, saying, ³"There is a covenant between me and you, as there was between my father and your father. Behold, I am sending to you silver and gold. Go, break your covenant with Baasha king of Israel, that he may withdraw from me." ⁴And Ben-hadad listened to King Asa and

sent the commanders of his armies against the cities of Israel, and they conquered Ijon, Dan, Abel-maim, and all the store cities of Naphtali. ⁵And when Baasha heard of it, he stopped building Ramah and let his work cease. ⁶Then King Asa took all Judah, and they carried away the stones of Ramah and its timber, with which Baasha had been building, and with them he built Geba and Mizpah.

⁷At that time Hanani the seer came to Asa king of Judah and said to him, "Because you relied on the king of Syria, and did not rely on the Lord your God, the army of the king of Syria has escaped you. ⁸Were not the Ethiopians and the Libyans a huge army with very many chariots and horsemen? Yet because you relied on the Lord, he gave them into your hand. ⁹For the eyes of the Lord run to and fro throughout the whole earth, to give strong support to those whose heart is blameless toward him. You have done foolishly in this, for from now on you will have wars." ¹⁰Then Asa was angry with the seer and put him in the stocks in prison, for he was in a rage with him because of this. And Asa inflicted cruelties upon some of the people at the same time.

¹¹The acts of Asa, from first to last, are written in the Book of the Kings of Judah and Israel. ¹²In the thirty-ninth year of his reign Asa was diseased in his feet, and his disease became severe. Yet even in his disease he did not seek the Lord, but sought help from physicians. ¹³And Asa slept with his fathers, dying in the forty-first year of his reign. ¹⁴They buried him in the tomb that he had cut for himself in the city of David. They laid him on a bier that had been filled with various kinds of spices prepared by the perfumer's art, and they made a very great fire in his honor.

Jehoshaphat Reigns in Judah

17 Jehoshaphat his son reigned in his place and strengthened himself against Israel. ² He placed forces in all the fortified cities of Judah and set garrisons in the land of Judah, and in the cities of Ephraim that Asa his father had captured. ³ The LORD was with Jehoshaphat, because he walked in the earlier ways of his father David. He did not seek the Baals, ⁴ but sought the God of his father and walked in his commandments, and not according to the practices of Israel. ⁵ Therefore the LORD established the kingdom in his hand. And all Judah brought tribute to Jehoshaphat, and he had great riches and honor. ⁶ His heart was courageous in the ways of the LORD. And furthermore, he took the high places and the Asherim out of Judah.

⁷ In the third year of his reign he sent his officials, Ben-hail, Obadiah, Zechariah, Nethanel, and Micaiah, to teach in the cities of Judah; ⁸ and with them the Levites, Shemaiah, Nethaniah, Zebadiah, Asahel, Shemiramoth, Jehonathan, Adonijah, Tobijah, and Tobadonijah; and with these Levites, the priests Elishama and Jehoram. ⁹ And they taught in Judah, having the Book of the Law of the LORD with them. They went about through all the cities of Judah and taught among the people.

¹⁰ And the fear of the LORD fell upon all the kingdoms of the lands that were around Judah, and they made no war against Jehoshaphat. ¹¹ Some of the Philistines brought Jehoshaphat presents and silver for tribute, and the Arabians also brought him 7,700 rams and 7,700 goats. ¹² And Jehoshaphat grew steadily greater. He built in Judah fortresses and store cities, ¹³ and he had large supplies in the cities of Judah. He had soldiers, mighty men of valor, in Jerusalem. ¹⁴ This was the muster

of them by fathers' houses: Of Judah, the commanders of thousands: Adnah the commander, with 300,000 mighty men of valor; ¹⁵ and next to him Jehohanan the commander, with 280,000; ¹⁶ and next to him Amasiah the son of Zichri, a volunteer for the service of the LORD, with 200,000 mighty men of valor. ¹⁷ Of Benjamin: Eliada, a mighty man of valor, with 200,000 men armed with bow and shield; ¹⁸ and next to him Jehozabad with 180,000 armed for war. ¹⁹ These were in the service of the king, besides those whom the king had placed in the fortified cities throughout all Judah.

Jehoshaphat Allies with Ahab

18 Now Jehoshaphat had great riches and honor, and he made a marriage alliance with Ahab. ² After some years he went down to Ahab in Samaria. And Ahab killed an abundance of sheep and oxen for him and for the people who were with him, and induced him to go up against Ramoth-gilead. ³ Ahab king of Israel said to Jehoshaphat king of Judah, "Will you go with me to Ramoth-gilead?" He answered him, "I am as you are, my people as your people. We will be with you in the war."

⁴ And Jehoshaphat said to the king of Israel, "Inquire first for the word of the LORD." ⁵ Then the king of Israel gathered the prophets together, four hundred men, and said to them, "Shall we go to battle against Ramoth-gilead, or shall I refrain?" And they said, "Go up, for God will give it into the hand of the king." ⁶ But Jehoshaphat said, "Is there not here another prophet of the LORD of whom we may inquire?" ⁷ And the king of Israel said to Jehoshaphat, "There is yet one man by whom we may inquire of the LORD, Micaiah the son of Imlah; but I

hate him, for he never prophesies good concerning me, but always evil." And Jehoshaphat said, "Let not the king say so." ⁸ Then the king of Israel summoned an officer and said, "Bring quickly Micaiah the son of Imlah." ⁹ Now the king of Israel and Jehoshaphat the king of Judah were sitting on their thrones, arrayed in their robes. And they were sitting at the threshing floor at the entrance of the gate of Samaria, and all the prophets were prophesying before them. ¹⁰ And Zedekiah the son of Chenaanah made for himself horns of iron and said, "Thus says the LORD, 'With these you shall push the Syrians until they are destroyed.'" ¹¹ And all the prophets prophesied so and said, "Go up to Ramoth-gilead and triumph. The LORD will give it into the hand of the king."

¹² And the messenger who went to summon Micaiah said to him, "Behold, the words of the prophets with one accord are favorable to the king. Let your word be like the word of one of them, and speak favorably." ¹³ But Micaiah said, "As the LORD lives, what my God says, that I will speak." ¹⁴ And when he had come to the king, the king said to him, "Micaiah, shall we go to Ramoth-gilead to battle, or shall I refrain?" And he answered, "Go up and triumph; they will be given into your hand." ¹⁵ But the king said to him, "How many times shall I make you swear that you speak to me nothing but the truth in the name of the LORD?" ¹⁶ And he said, "I saw all Israel scattered on the mountains, as sheep that have no shepherd. And the LORD said, 'These have no master; let each return to his home in peace.'" ¹⁷ And the king of Israel said to Jehoshaphat, "Did I not tell you that he would not prophesy good concerning me, but evil?" ¹⁸ And Micaiah said, "Therefore hear the word of the LORD: I saw the LORD sitting on his throne, and all the host of

heaven standing on his right hand and on his left. ¹⁹ And the LORD said, 'Who will entice Ahab the king of Israel, that he may go up and fall at Ramoth-gilead?' And one said one thing, and another said another. ²⁰ Then a spirit came forward and stood before the LORD, saying, 'I will entice him.' And the LORD said to him, 'By what means?' ²¹ And he said, 'I will go out, and will be a lying spirit in the mouth of all his prophets.' And he said, 'You are to entice him, and you shall succeed; go out and do so.' ²² Now therefore behold, the LORD has put a lying spirit in the mouth of these your prophets. The LORD has declared disaster concerning you."

²³ Then Zedekiah the son of Chenaanah came near and struck Micaiah on the cheek and said, "Which way did the Spirit of the LORD go from me to speak to you?" ²⁴ And Micaiah said, "Behold, you shall see on that day when you go into an inner chamber to hide yourself." ²⁵ And the king of Israel said, "Seize Micaiah and take him back to Amon the governor of the city and to Joash the king's son, ²⁶ and say, 'Thus says the king, Put this fellow in prison and feed him with meager rations of bread and water until I return in peace.'" ²⁷ And Micaiah said, "If you return in peace, the LORD has not spoken by me." And he said, "Hear, all you peoples!"

The Defeat and Death of Ahab

²⁸ So the king of Israel and Jehoshaphat the king of Judah went up to Ramoth-gilead. ²⁹ And the king of Israel said to Jehoshaphat, "I will disguise myself and go into battle, but you wear your robes." And the king of Israel disguised himself, and they went into battle. ³⁰ Now the king of Syria had commanded the captains of his chariots, "Fight with neither

small nor great, but only with the king of Israel." ³¹ As soon as the captains of the chariots saw Jehoshaphat, they said, "It is the king of Israel." So they turned to fight against him. And Jehoshaphat cried out, and the LORD helped him; God drew them away from him. ³² For as soon as the captains of the chariots saw that it was not the king of Israel, they turned back from pursuing him. ³³ But a certain man drew his bow at random and struck the king of Israel between the scale armor and the breastplate. Therefore he said to the driver of his chariot, "Turn around and carry me out of the battle, for I am wounded." ³⁴ And the battle continued that day, and the king of Israel was propped up in his chariot facing the Syrians until evening. Then at sunset he died.

Jehoshaphat's Reforms

19 Jehoshaphat the king of Judah returned in safety to his house in Jerusalem. ² But Jehu the son of Hanani the seer went out to meet him and said to King Jehoshaphat, "Should you help the wicked and love those who hate the LORD? Because of this, wrath has gone out against you from the LORD. ³ Nevertheless, some good is found in you, for you destroyed the Asheroth out of the land, and have set your heart to seek God."

⁴ Jehoshaphat lived at Jerusalem. And he went out again among the people, from Beersheba to the hill country of Ephraim, and brought them back to the LORD, the God of their fathers. ⁵ He appointed judges in the land in all the fortified cities of Judah, city by city, ⁶ and said to the judges, "Consider what you do, for you judge not for man but for the LORD. He is with you in giving judgment. ⁷ Now then, let the fear of the

LORD be upon you. Be careful what you do, for there is no injustice with the LORD our God, or partiality or taking bribes."

⁸ Moreover, in Jerusalem Jehoshaphat appointed certain Levites and priests and heads of families of Israel, to give judgment for the LORD and to decide disputed cases. They had their seat at Jerusalem. ⁹ And he charged them: "Thus you shall do in the fear of the LORD, in faithfulness, and with your whole heart: ¹⁰ whenever a case comes to you from your brothers who live in their cities, concerning bloodshed, law or commandment, statutes or rules, then you shall warn them, that they may not incur guilt before the LORD and wrath may not come upon you and your brothers. Thus you shall do, and you will not incur guilt. ¹¹ And behold, Amariah the chief priest is over you in all matters of the LORD; and Zebadiah the son of Ishmael, the governor of the house of Judah, in all the king's matters, and the Levites will serve you as officers. Deal courageously, and may the LORD be with the upright!"

Jehoshaphat's Prayer

20 After this the Moabites and Ammonites, and with them some of the Meunites, came against Jehoshaphat for battle. ² Some men came and told Jehoshaphat, "A great multitude is coming against you from Edom, from beyond the sea; and, behold, they are in Hazazon-tamar" (that is, Engedi). ³ Then Jehoshaphat was afraid and set his face to seek the LORD, and proclaimed a fast throughout all Judah. ⁴ And Judah assembled to seek help from the LORD; from all the cities of Judah they came to seek the LORD.

⁵ And Jehoshaphat stood in the assembly of Judah and Jerusalem, in the house of the LORD, before the new court, ⁶ and

said, "O Lord, God of our fathers, are you not God in heaven? You rule over all the kingdoms of the nations. In your hand are power and might, so that none is able to withstand you. ⁷ Did you not, our God, drive out the inhabitants of this land before your people Israel, and give it forever to the descendants of Abraham your friend? ⁸ And they have lived in it and have built for you in it a sanctuary for your name, saying, ⁹ 'If disaster comes upon us, the sword, judgment, or pestilence, or famine, we will stand before this house and before you—for your name is in this house—and cry out to you in our affliction, and you will hear and save.' ¹⁰ And now behold, the men of Ammon and Moab and Mount Seir, whom you would not let Israel invade when they came from the land of Egypt, and whom they avoided and did not destroy— ¹¹ behold, they reward us by coming to drive us out of your possession, which you have given us to inherit. ¹² O our God, will you not execute judgment on them? For we are powerless against this great horde that is coming against us. We do not know what to do, but our eyes are on you."

¹³ Meanwhile all Judah stood before the Lord, with their little ones, their wives, and their children. ¹⁴ And the Spirit of the Lord came upon Jahaziel the son of Zechariah, son of Benaiah, son of Jeiel, son of Mattaniah, a Levite of the sons of Asaph, in the midst of the assembly. ¹⁵ And he said, "Listen, all Judah and inhabitants of Jerusalem and King Jehoshaphat: Thus says the Lord to you, 'Do not be afraid and do not be dismayed at this great horde, for the battle is not yours but God's. ¹⁶ Tomorrow go down against them. Behold, they will come up by the ascent of Ziz. You will find them at the end of the valley, east of the wilderness of Jeruel. ¹⁷ You will not need to fight in this battle. Stand firm, hold your position, and see the salvation of the

LORD on your behalf, O Judah and Jerusalem.' Do not be afraid and do not be dismayed. Tomorrow go out against them, and the LORD will be with you."

¹⁸ Then Jehoshaphat bowed his head with his face to the ground, and all Judah and the inhabitants of Jerusalem fell down before the LORD, worshiping the LORD. ¹⁹ And the Levites, of the Kohathites and the Korahites, stood up to praise the LORD, the God of Israel, with a very loud voice.

²⁰ And they rose early in the morning and went out into the wilderness of Tekoa. And when they went out, Jehoshaphat stood and said, "Hear me, Judah and inhabitants of Jerusalem! Believe in the LORD your God, and you will be established; believe his prophets, and you will succeed." ²¹ And when he had taken counsel with the people, he appointed those who were to sing to the LORD and praise him in holy attire, as they went before the army, and say,

> "Give thanks to the LORD,
>   for his steadfast love endures forever."

²² And when they began to sing and praise, the LORD set an ambush against the men of Ammon, Moab, and Mount Seir, who had come against Judah, so that they were routed. ²³ For the men of Ammon and Moab rose against the inhabitants of Mount Seir, devoting them to destruction, and when they had made an end of the inhabitants of Seir, they all helped to destroy one another.

The LORD Delivers Judah

²⁴ When Judah came to the watchtower of the wilderness, they looked toward the horde, and behold, there were

dead bodies lying on the ground; none had escaped. ²⁵ When Jehoshaphat and his people came to take their spoil, they found among them, in great numbers, goods, clothing, and precious things, which they took for themselves until they could carry no more. They were three days in taking the spoil, it was so much. ²⁶ On the fourth day they assembled in the Valley of Beracah, for there they blessed the LORD. Therefore the name of that place has been called the Valley of Beracah to this day. ²⁷ Then they returned, every man of Judah and Jerusalem, and Jehoshaphat at their head, returning to Jerusalem with joy, for the LORD had made them rejoice over their enemies. ²⁸ They came to Jerusalem with harps and lyres and trumpets, to the house of the LORD. ²⁹ And the fear of God came on all the kingdoms of the countries when they heard that the LORD had fought against the enemies of Israel. ³⁰ So the realm of Jehoshaphat was quiet, for his God gave him rest all around.

³¹ Thus Jehoshaphat reigned over Judah. He was thirty-five years old when he began to reign, and he reigned twenty-five years in Jerusalem. His mother's name was Azubah the daughter of Shilhi. ³² He walked in the way of Asa his father and did not turn aside from it, doing what was right in the sight of the LORD. ³³ The high places, however, were not taken away; the people had not yet set their hearts upon the God of their fathers.

³⁴ Now the rest of the acts of Jehoshaphat, from first to last, are written in the chronicles of Jehu the son of Hanani, which are recorded in the Book of the Kings of Israel.

The End of Jehoshaphat's Reign

³⁵ After this Jehoshaphat king of Judah joined with Ahaziah king of Israel, who acted wickedly. ³⁶ He joined him in

building ships to go to Tarshish, and they built the ships in Ezion-geber. ³⁷ Then Eliezer the son of Dodavahu of Mareshah prophesied against Jehoshaphat, saying, "Because you have joined with Ahaziah, the LORD will destroy what you have made." And the ships were wrecked and were not able to go to Tarshish.

Jehoram Reigns in Judah

21 Jehoshaphat slept with his fathers and was buried with his fathers in the city of David, and Jehoram his son reigned in his place. ² He had brothers, the sons of Jehoshaphat: Azariah, Jehiel, Zechariah, Azariah, Michael, and Shephatiah; all these were the sons of Jehoshaphat king of Israel. ³ Their father gave them great gifts of silver, gold, and valuable possessions, together with fortified cities in Judah, but he gave the kingdom to Jehoram, because he was the firstborn. ⁴ When Jehoram had ascended the throne of his father and was established, he killed all his brothers with the sword, and also some of the princes of Israel. ⁵ Jehoram was thirty-two years old when he became king, and he reigned eight years in Jerusalem. ⁶ And he walked in the way of the kings of Israel, as the house of Ahab had done, for the daughter of Ahab was his wife. And he did what was evil in the sight of the LORD. ⁷ Yet the LORD was not willing to destroy the house of David, because of the covenant that he had made with David, and since he had promised to give a lamp to him and to his sons forever.

⁸ In his days Edom revolted from the rule of Judah and set up a king of their own. ⁹ Then Jehoram passed over with his commanders and all his chariots, and he rose by night and struck the Edomites who had surrounded him and his chariot

commanders. ¹⁰ So Edom revolted from the rule of Judah to this day. At that time Libnah also revolted from his rule, because he had forsaken the LORD, the God of his fathers.

¹¹ Moreover, he made high places in the hill country of Judah and led the inhabitants of Jerusalem into whoredom and made Judah go astray. ¹² And a letter came to him from Elijah the prophet, saying, "Thus says the LORD, the God of David your father, 'Because you have not walked in the ways of Jehoshaphat your father, or in the ways of Asa king of Judah, ¹³ but have walked in the way of the kings of Israel and have enticed Judah and the inhabitants of Jerusalem into whoredom, as the house of Ahab led Israel into whoredom, and also you have killed your brothers, of your father's house, who were better than you, ¹⁴ behold, the LORD will bring a great plague on your people, your children, your wives, and all your possessions, ¹⁵ and you yourself will have a severe sickness with a disease of your bowels, until your bowels come out because of the disease, day by day.'"

¹⁶ And the LORD stirred up against Jehoram the anger of the Philistines and of the Arabians who are near the Ethiopians. ¹⁷ And they came up against Judah and invaded it and carried away all the possessions they found that belonged to the king's house, and also his sons and his wives, so that no son was left to him except Jehoahaz, his youngest son.

¹⁸ And after all this the LORD struck him in his bowels with an incurable disease. ¹⁹ In the course of time, at the end of two years, his bowels came out because of the disease, and he died in great agony. His people made no fire in his honor, like the fires made for his fathers. ²⁰ He was thirty-two years old when he began to reign, and he reigned eight years in Jerusalem. And

he departed with no one's regret. They buried him in the city of David, but not in the tombs of the kings.

Ahaziah Reigns in Judah

22 And the inhabitants of Jerusalem made Ahaziah, his youngest son, king in his place, for the band of men that came with the Arabians to the camp had killed all the older sons. So Ahaziah the son of Jehoram king of Judah reigned. ² Ahaziah was twenty-two years old when he began to reign, and he reigned one year in Jerusalem. His mother's name was Athaliah, the granddaughter of Omri. ³ He also walked in the ways of the house of Ahab, for his mother was his counselor in doing wickedly. ⁴ He did what was evil in the sight of the LORD, as the house of Ahab had done. For after the death of his father they were his counselors, to his undoing. ⁵ He even followed their counsel and went with Jehoram the son of Ahab king of Israel to make war against Hazael king of Syria at Ramoth-gilead. And the Syrians wounded Joram, ⁶ and he returned to be healed in Jezreel of the wounds that he had received at Ramah, when he fought against Hazael king of Syria. And Ahaziah the son of Jehoram king of Judah went down to see Joram the son of Ahab in Jezreel, because he was wounded.

⁷ But it was ordained by God that the downfall of Ahaziah should come about through his going to visit Joram. For when he came there, he went out with Jehoram to meet Jehu the son of Nimshi, whom the LORD had anointed to destroy the house of Ahab. ⁸ And when Jehu was executing judgment on the house of Ahab, he met the princes of Judah and the sons of Ahaziah's brothers, who attended Ahaziah, and he killed them. ⁹ He searched for Ahaziah, and he was captured while hiding in

Samaria, and he was brought to Jehu and put to death. They buried him, for they said, "He is the grandson of Jehoshaphat, who sought the LORD with all his heart." And the house of Ahaziah had no one able to rule the kingdom.

Athaliah Reigns in Judah

¹⁰ Now when Athaliah the mother of Ahaziah saw that her son was dead, she arose and destroyed all the royal family of the house of Judah. ¹¹ But Jehoshabeath, the daughter of the king, took Joash the son of Ahaziah and stole him away from among the king's sons who were about to be put to death, and she put him and his nurse in a bedroom. Thus Jehoshabeath, the daughter of King Jehoram and wife of Jehoiada the priest, because she was a sister of Ahaziah, hid him from Athaliah, so that she did not put him to death. ¹² And he remained with them six years, hidden in the house of God, while Athaliah reigned over the land.

Joash Made King

23 But in the seventh year Jehoiada took courage and entered into a covenant with the commanders of hundreds, Azariah the son of Jeroham, Ishmael the son of Jehohanan, Azariah the son of Obed, Maaseiah the son of Adaiah, and Elishaphat the son of Zichri. ² And they went about through Judah and gathered the Levites from all the cities of Judah, and the heads of fathers' houses of Israel, and they came to Jerusalem. ³ And all the assembly made a covenant with the king in the house of God. And Jehoiada said to them, "Behold, the king's son! Let him reign, as the LORD spoke concerning the sons of David. ⁴ This is the thing that you shall do: of you priests and

Levites who come off duty on the Sabbath, one third shall be gatekeepers, ⁵and one third shall be at the king's house and one third at the Gate of the Foundation. And all the people shall be in the courts of the house of the LORD. ⁶Let no one enter the house of the LORD except the priests and ministering Levites. They may enter, for they are holy, but all the people shall keep the charge of the LORD. ⁷The Levites shall surround the king, each with his weapons in his hand. And whoever enters the house shall be put to death. Be with the king when he comes in and when he goes out."

⁸The Levites and all Judah did according to all that Jehoiada the priest commanded, and they each brought his men, who were to go off duty on the Sabbath, with those who were to come on duty on the Sabbath, for Jehoiada the priest did not dismiss the divisions. ⁹And Jehoiada the priest gave to the captains the spears and the large and small shields that had been King David's, which were in the house of God. ¹⁰And he set all the people as a guard for the king, every man with his weapon in his hand, from the south side of the house to the north side of the house, around the altar and the house. ¹¹Then they brought out the king's son and put the crown on him and gave him the testimony. And they proclaimed him king, and Jehoiada and his sons anointed him, and they said, "Long live the king."

Athaliah Executed

¹²When Athaliah heard the noise of the people running and praising the king, she went into the house of the LORD to the people. ¹³And when she looked, there was the king standing by his pillar at the entrance, and the captains and

the trumpeters beside the king, and all the people of the land rejoicing and blowing trumpets, and the singers with their musical instruments leading in the celebration. And Athaliah tore her clothes and cried, "Treason! Treason!" ¹⁴ Then Jehoiada the priest brought out the captains who were set over the army, saying to them, "Bring her out between the ranks, and anyone who follows her is to be put to death with the sword." For the priest said, "Do not put her to death in the house of the LORD." ¹⁵ So they laid hands on her, and she went into the entrance of the horse gate of the king's house, and they put her to death there.

Jehoiada's Reforms

¹⁶ And Jehoiada made a covenant between himself and all the people and the king that they should be the LORD's people. ¹⁷ Then all the people went to the house of Baal and tore it down; his altars and his images they broke in pieces, and they killed Mattan the priest of Baal before the altars. ¹⁸ And Jehoiada posted watchmen for the house of the LORD under the direction of the Levitical priests and the Levites whom David had organized to be in charge of the house of the LORD, to offer burnt offerings to the LORD, as it is written in the Law of Moses, with rejoicing and with singing, according to the order of David. ¹⁹ He stationed the gatekeepers at the gates of the house of the LORD so that no one should enter who was in any way unclean. ²⁰ And he took the captains, the nobles, the governors of the people, and all the people of the land, and they brought the king down from the house of the LORD, marching through the upper gate to the king's house. And they set the king on the royal throne. ²¹ So all the people of the

land rejoiced, and the city was quiet after Athaliah had been put to death with the sword.

Joash Repairs the Temple

24 Joash was seven years old when he began to reign, and he reigned forty years in Jerusalem. His mother's name was Zibiah of Beersheba. ²And Joash did what was right in the eyes of the LORD all the days of Jehoiada the priest. ³Jehoiada got for him two wives, and he had sons and daughters.

⁴After this Joash decided to restore the house of the LORD. ⁵And he gathered the priests and the Levites and said to them, "Go out to the cities of Judah and gather from all Israel money to repair the house of your God from year to year, and see that you act quickly." But the Levites did not act quickly. ⁶So the king summoned Jehoiada the chief and said to him, "Why have you not required the Levites to bring in from Judah and Jerusalem the tax levied by Moses, the servant of the LORD, and the congregation of Israel for the tent of testimony?" ⁷For the sons of Athaliah, that wicked woman, had broken into the house of God, and had also used all the dedicated things of the house of the LORD for the Baals.

⁸So the king commanded, and they made a chest and set it outside the gate of the house of the LORD. ⁹And proclamation was made throughout Judah and Jerusalem to bring in for the LORD the tax that Moses the servant of God laid on Israel in the wilderness. ¹⁰And all the princes and all the people rejoiced and brought their tax and dropped it into the chest until they had finished. ¹¹And whenever the chest was brought to the king's officers by the Levites, when they saw that there was much money in it, the king's secretary and the officer of the chief

priest would come and empty the chest and take it and return it to its place. Thus they did day after day, and collected money in abundance. ¹²And the king and Jehoiada gave it to those who had charge of the work of the house of the LORD, and they hired masons and carpenters to restore the house of the LORD, and also workers in iron and bronze to repair the house of the LORD. ¹³So those who were engaged in the work labored, and the repairing went forward in their hands, and they restored the house of God to its proper condition and strengthened it. ¹⁴And when they had finished, they brought the rest of the money before the king and Jehoiada, and with it were made utensils for the house of the LORD, both for the service and for the burnt offerings, and dishes for incense and vessels of gold and silver. And they offered burnt offerings in the house of the LORD regularly all the days of Jehoiada.

¹⁵But Jehoiada grew old and full of days, and died. He was 130 years old at his death. ¹⁶And they buried him in the city of David among the kings, because he had done good in Israel, and toward God and his house.

¹⁷Now after the death of Jehoiada the princes of Judah came and paid homage to the king. Then the king listened to them. ¹⁸And they abandoned the house of the LORD, the God of their fathers, and served the Asherim and the idols. And wrath came upon Judah and Jerusalem for this guilt of theirs. ¹⁹Yet he sent prophets among them to bring them back to the LORD. These testified against them, but they would not pay attention.

Joash's Treachery

²⁰Then the Spirit of God clothed Zechariah the son of Jehoiada the priest, and he stood above the people, and said

to them, "Thus says God, 'Why do you break the commandments of the LORD, so that you cannot prosper? Because you have forsaken the LORD, he has forsaken you.'" ²¹ But they conspired against him, and by command of the king they stoned him with stones in the court of the house of the LORD. ²² Thus Joash the king did not remember the kindness that Jehoiada, Zechariah's father, had shown him, but killed his son. And when he was dying, he said, "May the LORD see and avenge!"

Joash Assassinated

²³ At the end of the year the army of the Syrians came up against Joash. They came to Judah and Jerusalem and destroyed all the princes of the people from among the people and sent all their spoil to the king of Damascus. ²⁴ Though the army of the Syrians had come with few men, the LORD delivered into their hand a very great army, because Judah had forsaken the LORD, the God of their fathers. Thus they executed judgment on Joash.

²⁵ When they had departed from him, leaving him severely wounded, his servants conspired against him because of the blood of the son of Jehoiada the priest, and killed him on his bed. So he died, and they buried him in the city of David, but they did not bury him in the tombs of the kings. ²⁶ Those who conspired against him were Zabad the son of Shimeath the Ammonite, and Jehozabad the son of Shimrith the Moabite. ²⁷ Accounts of his sons and of the many oracles against him and of the rebuilding of the house of God are written in the Story of the Book of the Kings. And Amaziah his son reigned in his place.

Amaziah Reigns in Judah

25 Amaziah was twenty-five years old when he began to reign, and he reigned twenty-nine years in Jerusalem. His mother's name was Jehoaddan of Jerusalem. ²And he did what was right in the eyes of the LORD, yet not with a whole heart. ³And as soon as the royal power was firmly his, he killed his servants who had struck down the king his father. ⁴But he did not put their children to death, according to what is written in the Law, in the Book of Moses, where the LORD commanded, "Fathers shall not die because of their children, nor children die because of their fathers, but each one shall die for his own sin."

Amaziah's Victories

⁵Then Amaziah assembled the men of Judah and set them by fathers' houses under commanders of thousands and of hundreds for all Judah and Benjamin. He mustered those twenty years old and upward, and found that they were 300,000 choice men, fit for war, able to handle spear and shield. ⁶He hired also 100,000 mighty men of valor from Israel for 100 talents of silver. ⁷But a man of God came to him and said, "O king, do not let the army of Israel go with you, for the LORD is not with Israel, with all these Ephraimites. ⁸But go, act, be strong for the battle. Why should you suppose that God will cast you down before the enemy? For God has power to help or to cast down." ⁹And Amaziah said to the man of God, "But what shall we do about the hundred talents that I have given to the army of Israel?" The man of God answered, "The LORD is able to give you much more than this." ¹⁰Then Amaziah discharged the army that had come to him from Ephraim to go home again. And they became very angry with Judah and returned home in fierce anger. ¹¹But

Amaziah took courage and led out his people and went to the Valley of Salt and struck down 10,000 men of Seir. ¹² The men of Judah captured another 10,000 alive and took them to the top of a rock and threw them down from the top of the rock, and they were all dashed to pieces. ¹³ But the men of the army whom Amaziah sent back, not letting them go with him to battle, raided the cities of Judah, from Samaria to Beth-horon, and struck down 3,000 people in them and took much spoil.

Amaziah's Idolatry

¹⁴ After Amaziah came from striking down the Edomites, he brought the gods of the men of Seir and set them up as his gods and worshiped them, making offerings to them. ¹⁵ Therefore the LORD was angry with Amaziah and sent to him a prophet, who said to him, "Why have you sought the gods of a people who did not deliver their own people from your hand?" ¹⁶ But as he was speaking, the king said to him, "Have we made you a royal counselor? Stop! Why should you be struck down?" So the prophet stopped, but said, "I know that God has determined to destroy you, because you have done this and have not listened to my counsel."

Israel Defeats Amaziah

¹⁷ Then Amaziah king of Judah took counsel and sent to Joash the son of Jehoahaz, son of Jehu, king of Israel, saying, "Come, let us look one another in the face." ¹⁸ And Joash the king of Israel sent word to Amaziah king of Judah, "A thistle on Lebanon sent to a cedar on Lebanon, saying, 'Give your daughter to my son for a wife,' and a wild beast of Lebanon passed by and trampled down the thistle. ¹⁹ You say, 'See, I have struck

down Edom,' and your heart has lifted you up in boastfulness. But now stay at home. Why should you provoke trouble so that you fall, you and Judah with you?"

²⁰ But Amaziah would not listen, for it was of God, in order that he might give them into the hand of their enemies, because they had sought the gods of Edom. ²¹ So Joash king of Israel went up, and he and Amaziah king of Judah faced one another in battle at Beth-shemesh, which belongs to Judah. ²² And Judah was defeated by Israel, and every man fled to his home. ²³ And Joash king of Israel captured Amaziah king of Judah, the son of Joash, son of Ahaziah, at Beth-shemesh, and brought him to Jerusalem and broke down the wall of Jerusalem for 400 cubits, from the Ephraim Gate to the Corner Gate. ²⁴ And he seized all the gold and silver, and all the vessels that were found in the house of God, in the care of Obed-edom. He seized also the treasuries of the king's house, also hostages, and he returned to Samaria.

²⁵ Amaziah the son of Joash, king of Judah, lived fifteen years after the death of Joash the son of Jehoahaz, king of Israel. ²⁶ Now the rest of the deeds of Amaziah, from first to last, are they not written in the Book of the Kings of Judah and Israel? ²⁷ From the time when he turned away from the LORD they made a conspiracy against him in Jerusalem, and he fled to Lachish. But they sent after him to Lachish and put him to death there. ²⁸ And they brought him upon horses, and he was buried with his fathers in the city of David.

Uzziah Reigns in Judah

26 And all the people of Judah took Uzziah, who was sixteen years old, and made him king instead of his father Amaziah. ² He built Eloth and restored it to Judah, after the

king slept with his fathers. ³Uzziah was sixteen years old when he began to reign, and he reigned fifty-two years in Jerusalem. His mother's name was Jecoliah of Jerusalem. ⁴And he did what was right in the eyes of the LORD, according to all that his father Amaziah had done. ⁵He set himself to seek God in the days of Zechariah, who instructed him in the fear of God, and as long as he sought the LORD, God made him prosper.

⁶He went out and made war against the Philistines and broke through the wall of Gath and the wall of Jabneh and the wall of Ashdod, and he built cities in the territory of Ashdod and elsewhere among the Philistines. ⁷God helped him against the Philistines and against the Arabians who lived in Gurbaal and against the Meunites. ⁸The Ammonites paid tribute to Uzziah, and his fame spread even to the border of Egypt, for he became very strong. ⁹Moreover, Uzziah built towers in Jerusalem at the Corner Gate and at the Valley Gate and at the Angle, and fortified them. ¹⁰And he built towers in the wilderness and cut out many cisterns, for he had large herds, both in the Shephelah and in the plain, and he had farmers and vinedressers in the hills and in the fertile lands, for he loved the soil. ¹¹Moreover, Uzziah had an army of soldiers, fit for war, in divisions according to the numbers in the muster made by Jeiel the secretary and Maaseiah the officer, under the direction of Hananiah, one of the king's commanders. ¹²The whole number of the heads of fathers' houses of mighty men of valor was 2,600. ¹³Under their command was an army of 307,500, who could make war with mighty power, to help the king against the enemy. ¹⁴And Uzziah prepared for all the army shields, spears, helmets, coats of mail, bows, and stones for slinging. ¹⁵In Jerusalem he made machines, invented by skillful men, to be on the towers and the

corners, to shoot arrows and great stones. And his fame spread far, for he was marvelously helped, till he was strong.

Uzziah's Pride and Punishment

[16] But when he was strong, he grew proud, to his destruction. For he was unfaithful to the LORD his God and entered the temple of the LORD to burn incense on the altar of incense. [17] But Azariah the priest went in after him, with eighty priests of the LORD who were men of valor, [18] and they withstood King Uzziah and said to him, "It is not for you, Uzziah, to burn incense to the LORD, but for the priests, the sons of Aaron, who are consecrated to burn incense. Go out of the sanctuary, for you have done wrong, and it will bring you no honor from the LORD God." [19] Then Uzziah was angry. Now he had a censer in his hand to burn incense, and when he became angry with the priests, leprosy broke out on his forehead in the presence of the priests in the house of the LORD, by the altar of incense. [20] And Azariah the chief priest and all the priests looked at him, and behold, he was leprous in his forehead! And they rushed him out quickly, and he himself hurried to go out, because the LORD had struck him. [21] And King Uzziah was a leper to the day of his death, and being a leper lived in a separate house, for he was excluded from the house of the LORD. And Jotham his son was over the king's household, governing the people of the land.

[22] Now the rest of the acts of Uzziah, from first to last, Isaiah the prophet the son of Amoz wrote. [23] And Uzziah slept with his fathers, and they buried him with his fathers in the burial field that belonged to the kings, for they said, "He is a leper." And Jotham his son reigned in his place.

Jotham Reigns in Judah

27 Jotham was twenty-five years old when he began to reign, and he reigned sixteen years in Jerusalem. His mother's name was Jerushah the daughter of Zadok. ²And he did what was right in the eyes of the LORD according to all that his father Uzziah had done, except he did not enter the temple of the LORD. But the people still followed corrupt practices. ³He built the upper gate of the house of the LORD and did much building on the wall of Ophel. ⁴Moreover, he built cities in the hill country of Judah, and forts and towers on the wooded hills. ⁵He fought with the king of the Ammonites and prevailed against them. And the Ammonites gave him that year 100 talents of silver, and 10,000 cors of wheat and 10,000 of barley. The Ammonites paid him the same amount in the second and the third years. ⁶So Jotham became mighty, because he ordered his ways before the LORD his God. ⁷Now the rest of the acts of Jotham, and all his wars and his ways, behold, they are written in the Book of the Kings of Israel and Judah. ⁸He was twenty-five years old when he began to reign, and he reigned sixteen years in Jerusalem. ⁹And Jotham slept with his fathers, and they buried him in the city of David, and Ahaz his son reigned in his place.

Ahaz Reigns in Judah

28 Ahaz was twenty years old when he began to reign, and he reigned sixteen years in Jerusalem. And he did not do what was right in the eyes of the LORD, as his father David had done, ²but he walked in the ways of the kings of Israel. He even made metal images for the Baals, ³and he made offerings in the Valley of the Son of Hinnom and burned his sons as an offering, according to the abominations of the nations whom

the LORD drove out before the people of Israel. ⁴And he sacrificed and made offerings on the high places and on the hills and under every green tree.

Judah Defeated

⁵Therefore the LORD his God gave him into the hand of the king of Syria, who defeated him and took captive a great number of his people and brought them to Damascus. He was also given into the hand of the king of Israel, who struck him with great force. ⁶For Pekah the son of Remaliah killed 120,000 from Judah in one day, all of them men of valor, because they had forsaken the LORD, the God of their fathers. ⁷And Zichri, a mighty man of Ephraim, killed Maaseiah the king's son and Azrikam the commander of the palace and Elkanah the next in authority to the king.

⁸The men of Israel took captive 200,000 of their relatives, women, sons, and daughters. They also took much spoil from them and brought the spoil to Samaria. ⁹But a prophet of the LORD was there, whose name was Oded, and he went out to meet the army that came to Samaria and said to them, "Behold, because the LORD, the God of your fathers, was angry with Judah, he gave them into your hand, but you have killed them in a rage that has reached up to heaven. ¹⁰And now you intend to subjugate the people of Judah and Jerusalem, male and female, as your slaves. Have you not sins of your own against the LORD your God? ¹¹Now hear me, and send back the captives from your relatives whom you have taken, for the fierce wrath of the LORD is upon you."

¹²Certain chiefs also of the men of Ephraim, Azariah the son of Johanan, Berechiah the son of Meshillemoth, Jehizkiah the

son of Shallum, and Amasa the son of Hadlai, stood up against those who were coming from the war [13] and said to them, "You shall not bring the captives in here, for you propose to bring upon us guilt against the LORD in addition to our present sins and guilt. For our guilt is already great, and there is fierce wrath against Israel." [14] So the armed men left the captives and the spoil before the princes and all the assembly. [15] And the men who have been mentioned by name rose and took the captives, and with the spoil they clothed all who were naked among them. They clothed them, gave them sandals, provided them with food and drink, and anointed them, and carrying all the feeble among them on donkeys, they brought them to their kinsfolk at Jericho, the city of palm trees. Then they returned to Samaria.

[16] At that time King Ahaz sent to the king of Assyria for help. [17] For the Edomites had again invaded and defeated Judah and carried away captives. [18] And the Philistines had made raids on the cities in the Shephelah and the Negeb of Judah, and had taken Beth-shemesh, Aijalon, Gederoth, Soco with its villages, Timnah with its villages, and Gimzo with its villages. And they settled there. [19] For the LORD humbled Judah because of Ahaz king of Israel, for he had made Judah act sinfully and had been very unfaithful to the LORD. [20] So Tiglath-pileser king of Assyria came against him and afflicted him instead of strengthening him. [21] For Ahaz took a portion from the house of the LORD and the house of the king and of the princes, and gave tribute to the king of Assyria, but it did not help him.

Ahaz's Idolatry

[22] In the time of his distress he became yet more faithless to the LORD—this same King Ahaz. [23] For he sacrificed to the

gods of Damascus that had defeated him and said, "Because the gods of the kings of Syria helped them, I will sacrifice to them that they may help me." But they were the ruin of him and of all Israel. ²⁴ And Ahaz gathered together the vessels of the house of God and cut in pieces the vessels of the house of God, and he shut up the doors of the house of the LORD, and he made himself altars in every corner of Jerusalem. ²⁵ In every city of Judah he made high places to make offerings to other gods, provoking to anger the LORD, the God of his fathers. ²⁶ Now the rest of his acts and all his ways, from first to last, behold, they are written in the Book of the Kings of Judah and Israel. ²⁷ And Ahaz slept with his fathers, and they buried him in the city, in Jerusalem, for they did not bring him into the tombs of the kings of Israel. And Hezekiah his son reigned in his place.

Hezekiah Reigns in Judah

29 Hezekiah began to reign when he was twenty-five years old, and he reigned twenty-nine years in Jerusalem. His mother's name was Abijah the daughter of Zechariah. ² And he did what was right in the eyes of the LORD, according to all that David his father had done.

Hezekiah Cleanses the Temple

³ In the first year of his reign, in the first month, he opened the doors of the house of the LORD and repaired them. ⁴ He brought in the priests and the Levites and assembled them in the square on the east ⁵ and said to them, "Hear me, Levites! Now consecrate yourselves, and consecrate the house of the LORD, the God of your fathers, and carry out the filth from the Holy Place. ⁶ For our fathers have been unfaithful and have

done what was evil in the sight of the LORD our God. They have forsaken him and have turned away their faces from the habitation of the LORD and turned their backs. ⁷ They also shut the doors of the vestibule and put out the lamps and have not burned incense or offered burnt offerings in the Holy Place to the God of Israel. ⁸ Therefore the wrath of the LORD came on Judah and Jerusalem, and he has made them an object of horror, of astonishment, and of hissing, as you see with your own eyes. ⁹ For behold, our fathers have fallen by the sword, and our sons and our daughters and our wives are in captivity for this. ¹⁰ Now it is in my heart to make a covenant with the LORD, the God of Israel, in order that his fierce anger may turn away from us. ¹¹ My sons, do not now be negligent, for the LORD has chosen you to stand in his presence, to minister to him and to be his ministers and make offerings to him."

¹² Then the Levites arose, Mahath the son of Amasai, and Joel the son of Azariah, of the sons of the Kohathites; and of the sons of Merari, Kish the son of Abdi, and Azariah the son of Jehallelel; and of the Gershonites, Joah the son of Zimmah, and Eden the son of Joah; ¹³ and of the sons of Elizaphan, Shimri and Jeuel; and of the sons of Asaph, Zechariah and Mattaniah; ¹⁴ and of the sons of Heman, Jehuel and Shimei; and of the sons of Jeduthun, Shemaiah and Uzziel. ¹⁵ They gathered their brothers and consecrated themselves and went in as the king had commanded, by the words of the LORD, to cleanse the house of the LORD. ¹⁶ The priests went into the inner part of the house of the LORD to cleanse it, and they brought out all the uncleanness that they found in the temple of the LORD into the court of the house of the LORD. And the Levites took it and carried it out to the brook Kidron. ¹⁷ They began to consecrate

on the first day of the first month, and on the eighth day of the month they came to the vestibule of the LORD. Then for eight days they consecrated the house of the LORD, and on the sixteenth day of the first month they finished. [18] Then they went in to Hezekiah the king and said, "We have cleansed all the house of the LORD, the altar of burnt offering and all its utensils, and the table for the showbread and all its utensils. [19] All the utensils that King Ahaz discarded in his reign when he was faithless, we have made ready and consecrated, and behold, they are before the altar of the LORD."

Hezekiah Restores Temple Worship

[20] Then Hezekiah the king rose early and gathered the officials of the city and went up to the house of the LORD. [21] And they brought seven bulls, seven rams, seven lambs, and seven male goats for a sin offering for the kingdom and for the sanctuary and for Judah. And he commanded the priests, the sons of Aaron, to offer them on the altar of the LORD. [22] So they slaughtered the bulls, and the priests received the blood and threw it against the altar. And they slaughtered the rams, and their blood was thrown against the altar. And they slaughtered the lambs, and their blood was thrown against the altar. [23] Then the goats for the sin offering were brought to the king and the assembly, and they laid their hands on them, [24] and the priests slaughtered them and made a sin offering with their blood on the altar, to make atonement for all Israel. For the king commanded that the burnt offering and the sin offering should be made for all Israel.

[25] And he stationed the Levites in the house of the LORD with cymbals, harps, and lyres, according to the commandment of

David and of Gad the king's seer and of Nathan the prophet, for the commandment was from the LORD through his prophets. ²⁶ The Levites stood with the instruments of David, and the priests with the trumpets. ²⁷ Then Hezekiah commanded that the burnt offering be offered on the altar. And when the burnt offering began, the song to the LORD began also, and the trumpets, accompanied by the instruments of David king of Israel. ²⁸ The whole assembly worshiped, and the singers sang, and the trumpeters sounded. All this continued until the burnt offering was finished. ²⁹ When the offering was finished, the king and all who were present with him bowed themselves and worshiped. ³⁰ And Hezekiah the king and the officials commanded the Levites to sing praises to the LORD with the words of David and of Asaph the seer. And they sang praises with gladness, and they bowed down and worshiped.

³¹ Then Hezekiah said, "You have now consecrated yourselves to the LORD. Come near; bring sacrifices and thank offerings to the house of the LORD." And the assembly brought sacrifices and thank offerings, and all who were of a willing heart brought burnt offerings. ³² The number of the burnt offerings that the assembly brought was 70 bulls, 100 rams, and 200 lambs; all these were for a burnt offering to the LORD. ³³ And the consecrated offerings were 600 bulls and 3,000 sheep. ³⁴ But the priests were too few and could not flay all the burnt offerings, so until other priests had consecrated themselves, their brothers the Levites helped them, until the work was finished—for the Levites were more upright in heart than the priests in consecrating themselves. ³⁵ Besides the great number of burnt offerings, there was the fat of the peace offerings, and there were the drink offerings for the burnt offerings. Thus the

service of the house of the LORD was restored. ³⁶ And Hezekiah and all the people rejoiced because God had provided for the people, for the thing came about suddenly.

Passover Celebrated

30 Hezekiah sent to all Israel and Judah, and wrote letters also to Ephraim and Manasseh, that they should come to the house of the LORD at Jerusalem to keep the Passover to the LORD, the God of Israel. ² For the king and his princes and all the assembly in Jerusalem had taken counsel to keep the Passover in the second month — ³ for they could not keep it at that time because the priests had not consecrated themselves in sufficient number, nor had the people assembled in Jerusalem — ⁴ and the plan seemed right to the king and all the assembly. ⁵ So they decreed to make a proclamation throughout all Israel, from Beersheba to Dan, that the people should come and keep the Passover to the LORD, the God of Israel, at Jerusalem, for they had not kept it as often as prescribed. ⁶ So couriers went throughout all Israel and Judah with letters from the king and his princes, as the king had commanded, saying, "O people of Israel, return to the LORD, the God of Abraham, Isaac, and Israel, that he may turn again to the remnant of you who have escaped from the hand of the kings of Assyria. ⁷ Do not be like your fathers and your brothers, who were faithless to the LORD God of their fathers, so that he made them a desolation, as you see. ⁸ Do not now be stiff-necked as your fathers were, but yield yourselves to the LORD and come to his sanctuary, which he has consecrated forever, and serve the LORD your God, that his fierce anger may turn away from you. ⁹ For if you return to the LORD, your brothers and your children will find

compassion with their captors and return to this land. For the LORD your God is gracious and merciful and will not turn away his face from you, if you return to him."

¹⁰ So the couriers went from city to city through the country of Ephraim and Manasseh, and as far as Zebulun, but they laughed them to scorn and mocked them. ¹¹ However, some men of Asher, of Manasseh, and of Zebulun humbled themselves and came to Jerusalem. ¹² The hand of God was also on Judah to give them one heart to do what the king and the princes commanded by the word of the LORD.

¹³ And many people came together in Jerusalem to keep the Feast of Unleavened Bread in the second month, a very great assembly. ¹⁴ They set to work and removed the altars that were in Jerusalem, and all the altars for burning incense they took away and threw into the brook Kidron. ¹⁵ And they slaughtered the Passover lamb on the fourteenth day of the second month. And the priests and the Levites were ashamed, so that they consecrated themselves and brought burnt offerings into the house of the LORD. ¹⁶ They took their accustomed posts according to the Law of Moses the man of God. The priests threw the blood that they received from the hand of the Levites. ¹⁷ For there were many in the assembly who had not consecrated themselves. Therefore the Levites had to slaughter the Passover lamb for everyone who was not clean, to consecrate it to the LORD. ¹⁸ For a majority of the people, many of them from Ephraim, Manasseh, Issachar, and Zebulun, had not cleansed themselves, yet they ate the Passover otherwise than as prescribed. For Hezekiah had prayed for them, saying, "May the good LORD pardon everyone ¹⁹ who sets his heart to seek God, the LORD, the God of his fathers, even though not according

to the sanctuary's rules of cleanness." ²⁰ And the LORD heard Hezekiah and healed the people. ²¹ And the people of Israel who were present at Jerusalem kept the Feast of Unleavened Bread seven days with great gladness, and the Levites and the priests praised the LORD day by day, singing with all their might to the LORD. ²² And Hezekiah spoke encouragingly to all the Levites who showed good skill in the service of the LORD. So they ate the food of the festival for seven days, sacrificing peace offerings and giving thanks to the LORD, the God of their fathers.

²³ Then the whole assembly agreed together to keep the feast for another seven days. So they kept it for another seven days with gladness. ²⁴ For Hezekiah king of Judah gave the assembly 1,000 bulls and 7,000 sheep for offerings, and the princes gave the assembly 1,000 bulls and 10,000 sheep. And the priests consecrated themselves in great numbers. ²⁵ The whole assembly of Judah, and the priests and the Levites, and the whole assembly that came out of Israel, and the sojourners who came out of the land of Israel, and the sojourners who lived in Judah, rejoiced. ²⁶ So there was great joy in Jerusalem, for since the time of Solomon the son of David king of Israel there had been nothing like this in Jerusalem. ²⁷ Then the priests and the Levites arose and blessed the people, and their voice was heard, and their prayer came to his holy habitation in heaven.

Hezekiah Organizes the Priests

31 Now when all this was finished, all Israel who were present went out to the cities of Judah and broke in pieces the pillars and cut down the Asherim and broke down the high places and the altars throughout all Judah and Benjamin, and

in Ephraim and Manasseh, until they had destroyed them all. Then all the people of Israel returned to their cities, every man to his possession.

²And Hezekiah appointed the divisions of the priests and of the Levites, division by division, each according to his service, the priests and the Levites, for burnt offerings and peace offerings, to minister in the gates of the camp of the LORD and to give thanks and praise. ³The contribution of the king from his own possessions was for the burnt offerings: the burnt offerings of morning and evening, and the burnt offerings for the Sabbaths, the new moons, and the appointed feasts, as it is written in the Law of the LORD. ⁴And he commanded the people who lived in Jerusalem to give the portion due to the priests and the Levites, that they might give themselves to the Law of the LORD. ⁵As soon as the command was spread abroad, the people of Israel gave in abundance the firstfruits of grain, wine, oil, honey, and of all the produce of the field. And they brought in abundantly the tithe of everything. ⁶And the people of Israel and Judah who lived in the cities of Judah also brought in the tithe of cattle and sheep, and the tithe of the dedicated things that had been dedicated to the LORD their God, and laid them in heaps. ⁷In the third month they began to pile up the heaps, and finished them in the seventh month. ⁸When Hezekiah and the princes came and saw the heaps, they blessed the LORD and his people Israel. ⁹And Hezekiah questioned the priests and the Levites about the heaps. ¹⁰Azariah the chief priest, who was of the house of Zadok, answered him, "Since they began to bring the contributions into the house of the LORD, we have eaten and had enough and have plenty left, for the LORD has blessed his people, so that we have this large amount left."

[11] Then Hezekiah commanded them to prepare chambers in the house of the LORD, and they prepared them. [12] And they faithfully brought in the contributions, the tithes, and the dedicated things. The chief officer in charge of them was Conaniah the Levite, with Shimei his brother as second, [13] while Jehiel, Azaziah, Nahath, Asahel, Jerimoth, Jozabad, Eliel, Ismachiah, Mahath, and Benaiah were overseers assisting Conaniah and Shimei his brother, by the appointment of Hezekiah the king and Azariah the chief officer of the house of God. [14] And Kore the son of Imnah the Levite, keeper of the east gate, was over the freewill offerings to God, to apportion the contribution reserved for the LORD and the most holy offerings. [15] Eden, Miniamin, Jeshua, Shemaiah, Amariah, and Shecaniah were faithfully assisting him in the cities of the priests, to distribute the portions to their brothers, old and young alike, by divisions, [16] except those enrolled by genealogy, males from three years old and upward—all who entered the house of the LORD as the duty of each day required—for their service according to their offices, by their divisions. [17] The enrollment of the priests was according to their fathers' houses; that of the Levites from twenty years old and upward was according to their offices, by their divisions. [18] They were enrolled with all their little children, their wives, their sons, and their daughters, the whole assembly, for they were faithful in keeping themselves holy. [19] And for the sons of Aaron, the priests, who were in the fields of common land belonging to their cities, there were men in the several cities who were designated by name to distribute portions to every male among the priests and to everyone among the Levites who was enrolled.

[20] Thus Hezekiah did throughout all Judah, and he did what was good and right and faithful before the LORD his God. [21] And

every work that he undertook in the service of the house of God and in accordance with the law and the commandments, seeking his God, he did with all his heart, and prospered.

Sennacherib Invades Judah

32 After these things and these acts of faithfulness, Sennacherib king of Assyria came and invaded Judah and encamped against the fortified cities, thinking to win them for himself. ² And when Hezekiah saw that Sennacherib had come and intended to fight against Jerusalem, ³ he planned with his officers and his mighty men to stop the water of the springs that were outside the city; and they helped him. ⁴ A great many people were gathered, and they stopped all the springs and the brook that flowed through the land, saying, "Why should the kings of Assyria come and find much water?" ⁵ He set to work resolutely and built up all the wall that was broken down and raised towers upon it, and outside it he built another wall, and he strengthened the Millo in the city of David. He also made weapons and shields in abundance. ⁶ And he set combat commanders over the people and gathered them together to him in the square at the gate of the city and spoke encouragingly to them, saying, ⁷ "Be strong and courageous. Do not be afraid or dismayed before the king of Assyria and all the horde that is with him, for there are more with us than with him. ⁸ With him is an arm of flesh, but with us is the LORD our God, to help us and to fight our battles." And the people took confidence from the words of Hezekiah king of Judah.

Sennacherib Blasphemes

⁹ After this, Sennacherib king of Assyria, who was besieging Lachish with all his forces, sent his servants to Jerusalem

to Hezekiah king of Judah and to all the people of Judah who were in Jerusalem, saying, [10] "Thus says Sennacherib king of Assyria, 'On what are you trusting, that you endure the siege in Jerusalem? [11] Is not Hezekiah misleading you, that he may give you over to die by famine and by thirst, when he tells you, "The LORD our God will deliver us from the hand of the king of Assyria"? [12] Has not this same Hezekiah taken away his high places and his altars and commanded Judah and Jerusalem, "Before one altar you shall worship, and on it you shall burn your sacrifices"? [13] Do you not know what I and my fathers have done to all the peoples of other lands? Were the gods of the nations of those lands at all able to deliver their lands out of my hand? [14] Who among all the gods of those nations that my fathers devoted to destruction was able to deliver his people from my hand, that your God should be able to deliver you from my hand? [15] Now, therefore, do not let Hezekiah deceive you or mislead you in this fashion, and do not believe him, for no god of any nation or kingdom has been able to deliver his people from my hand or from the hand of my fathers. How much less will your God deliver you out of my hand!'"

[16] And his servants said still more against the LORD God and against his servant Hezekiah. [17] And he wrote letters to cast contempt on the LORD, the God of Israel, and to speak against him, saying, "Like the gods of the nations of the lands who have not delivered their people from my hands, so the God of Hezekiah will not deliver his people from my hand." [18] And they shouted it with a loud voice in the language of Judah to the people of Jerusalem who were on the wall, to frighten and terrify them, in order that they might take the city. [19] And they spoke of the God of Jerusalem as they spoke

of the gods of the peoples of the earth, which are the work of men's hands.

The LORD Delivers Jerusalem

²⁰ Then Hezekiah the king and Isaiah the prophet, the son of Amoz, prayed because of this and cried to heaven. ²¹ And the LORD sent an angel, who cut off all the mighty warriors and commanders and officers in the camp of the king of Assyria. So he returned with shame of face to his own land. And when he came into the house of his god, some of his own sons struck him down there with the sword. ²² So the LORD saved Hezekiah and the inhabitants of Jerusalem from the hand of Sennacherib king of Assyria and from the hand of all his enemies, and he provided for them on every side. ²³ And many brought gifts to the LORD to Jerusalem and precious things to Hezekiah king of Judah, so that he was exalted in the sight of all nations from that time onward.

Hezekiah's Pride and Achievements

²⁴ In those days Hezekiah became sick and was at the point of death, and he prayed to the LORD, and he answered him and gave him a sign. ²⁵ But Hezekiah did not make return according to the benefit done to him, for his heart was proud. Therefore wrath came upon him and Judah and Jerusalem. ²⁶ But Hezekiah humbled himself for the pride of his heart, both he and the inhabitants of Jerusalem, so that the wrath of the LORD did not come upon them in the days of Hezekiah.

²⁷ And Hezekiah had very great riches and honor, and he made for himself treasuries for silver, for gold, for precious stones, for spices, for shields, and for all kinds of costly vessels;

[28] storehouses also for the yield of grain, wine, and oil; and stalls for all kinds of cattle, and sheepfolds. [29] He likewise provided cities for himself, and flocks and herds in abundance, for God had given him very great possessions. [30] This same Hezekiah closed the upper outlet of the waters of Gihon and directed them down to the west side of the city of David. And Hezekiah prospered in all his works. [31] And so in the matter of the envoys of the princes of Babylon, who had been sent to him to inquire about the sign that had been done in the land, God left him to himself, in order to test him and to know all that was in his heart.

[32] Now the rest of the acts of Hezekiah and his good deeds, behold, they are written in the vision of Isaiah the prophet, the son of Amoz, in the Book of the Kings of Judah and Israel. [33] And Hezekiah slept with his fathers, and they buried him in the upper part of the tombs of the sons of David, and all Judah and the inhabitants of Jerusalem did him honor at his death. And Manasseh his son reigned in his place.

Manasseh Reigns in Judah

33 Manasseh was twelve years old when he began to reign, and he reigned fifty-five years in Jerusalem. [2] And he did what was evil in the sight of the Lord, according to the abominations of the nations whom the Lord drove out before the people of Israel. [3] For he rebuilt the high places that his father Hezekiah had broken down, and he erected altars to the Baals, and made Asheroth, and worshiped all the host of heaven and served them. [4] And he built altars in the house of the Lord, of which the Lord had said, "In Jerusalem shall my name be forever." [5] And he built altars for all the host of heaven in the two courts of the house of the Lord. [6] And he burned his sons as an offering in the Valley

of the Son of Hinnom, and used fortune-telling and omens and sorcery, and dealt with mediums and with necromancers. He did much evil in the sight of the LORD, provoking him to anger. ⁷ And the carved image of the idol that he had made he set in the house of God, of which God said to David and to Solomon his son, "In this house, and in Jerusalem, which I have chosen out of all the tribes of Israel, I will put my name forever, ⁸ and I will no more remove the foot of Israel from the land that I appointed for your fathers, if only they will be careful to do all that I have commanded them, all the law, the statutes, and the rules given through Moses." ⁹ Manasseh led Judah and the inhabitants of Jerusalem astray, to do more evil than the nations whom the LORD destroyed before the people of Israel.

Manasseh's Repentance

¹⁰ The LORD spoke to Manasseh and to his people, but they paid no attention. ¹¹ Therefore the LORD brought upon them the commanders of the army of the king of Assyria, who captured Manasseh with hooks and bound him with chains of bronze and brought him to Babylon. ¹² And when he was in distress, he entreated the favor of the LORD his God and humbled himself greatly before the God of his fathers. ¹³ He prayed to him, and God was moved by his entreaty and heard his plea and brought him again to Jerusalem into his kingdom. Then Manasseh knew that the LORD was God.

¹⁴ Afterward he built an outer wall for the city of David west of Gihon, in the valley, and for the entrance into the Fish Gate, and carried it around Ophel, and raised it to a very great height. He also put commanders of the army in all the fortified cities in Judah. ¹⁵ And he took away the foreign gods and the idol from

the house of the LORD, and all the altars that he had built on the mountain of the house of the LORD and in Jerusalem, and he threw them outside of the city. ¹⁶ He also restored the altar of the LORD and offered on it sacrifices of peace offerings and of thanksgiving, and he commanded Judah to serve the LORD, the God of Israel. ¹⁷ Nevertheless, the people still sacrificed at the high places, but only to the LORD their God.

¹⁸ Now the rest of the acts of Manasseh, and his prayer to his God, and the words of the seers who spoke to him in the name of the LORD, the God of Israel, behold, they are in the Chronicles of the Kings of Israel. ¹⁹ And his prayer, and how God was moved by his entreaty, and all his sin and his faithlessness, and the sites on which he built high places and set up the Asherim and the images, before he humbled himself, behold, they are written in the Chronicles of the Seers. ²⁰ So Manasseh slept with his fathers, and they buried him in his house, and Amon his son reigned in his place.

Amon's Reign and Death

²¹ Amon was twenty-two years old when he began to reign, and he reigned two years in Jerusalem. ²² And he did what was evil in the sight of the LORD, as Manasseh his father had done. Amon sacrificed to all the images that Manasseh his father had made, and served them. ²³ And he did not humble himself before the LORD, as Manasseh his father had humbled himself, but this Amon incurred guilt more and more. ²⁴ And his servants conspired against him and put him to death in his house. ²⁵ But the people of the land struck down all those who had conspired against King Amon. And the people of the land made Josiah his son king in his place.

Josiah Reigns in Judah

34 Josiah was eight years old when he began to reign, and he reigned thirty-one years in Jerusalem. ²And he did what was right in the eyes of the LORD, and walked in the ways of David his father; and he did not turn aside to the right hand or to the left. ³For in the eighth year of his reign, while he was yet a boy, he began to seek the God of David his father, and in the twelfth year he began to purge Judah and Jerusalem of the high places, the Asherim, and the carved and the metal images. ⁴And they chopped down the altars of the Baals in his presence, and he cut down the incense altars that stood above them. And he broke in pieces the Asherim and the carved and the metal images, and he made dust of them and scattered it over the graves of those who had sacrificed to them. ⁵He also burned the bones of the priests on their altars and cleansed Judah and Jerusalem. ⁶And in the cities of Manasseh, Ephraim, and Simeon, and as far as Naphtali, in their ruins all around, ⁷he broke down the altars and beat the Asherim and the images into powder and cut down all the incense altars throughout all the land of Israel. Then he returned to Jerusalem.

The Book of the Law Found

⁸Now in the eighteenth year of his reign, when he had cleansed the land and the house, he sent Shaphan the son of Azaliah, and Maaseiah the governor of the city, and Joah the son of Joahaz, the recorder, to repair the house of the LORD his God. ⁹They came to Hilkiah the high priest and gave him the money that had been brought into the house of God, which the Levites, the keepers of the threshold, had collected from Manasseh and Ephraim and from all the remnant of Israel and from all Judah

and Benjamin and from the inhabitants of Jerusalem. ¹⁰And they gave it to the workmen who were working in the house of the LORD. And the workmen who were working in the house of the LORD gave it for repairing and restoring the house. ¹¹They gave it to the carpenters and the builders to buy quarried stone, and timber for binders and beams for the buildings that the kings of Judah had let go to ruin. ¹²And the men did the work faithfully. Over them were set Jahath and Obadiah the Levites, of the sons of Merari, and Zechariah and Meshullam, of the sons of the Kohathites, to have oversight. The Levites, all who were skillful with instruments of music, ¹³were over the burden-bearers and directed all who did work in every kind of service, and some of the Levites were scribes and officials and gatekeepers.

¹⁴While they were bringing out the money that had been brought into the house of the LORD, Hilkiah the priest found the Book of the Law of the LORD given through Moses. ¹⁵Then Hilkiah answered and said to Shaphan the secretary, "I have found the Book of the Law in the house of the LORD." And Hilkiah gave the book to Shaphan. ¹⁶Shaphan brought the book to the king, and further reported to the king, "All that was committed to your servants they are doing. ¹⁷They have emptied out the money that was found in the house of the LORD and have given it into the hand of the overseers and the workmen." ¹⁸Then Shaphan the secretary told the king, "Hilkiah the priest has given me a book." And Shaphan read from it before the king.

¹⁹And when the king heard the words of the Law, he tore his clothes. ²⁰And the king commanded Hilkiah, Ahikam the son of Shaphan, Abdon the son of Micah, Shaphan the secretary, and Asaiah the king's servant, saying, ²¹"Go, inquire of the

Lord for me and for those who are left in Israel and in Judah, concerning the words of the book that has been found. For great is the wrath of the Lord that is poured out on us, because our fathers have not kept the word of the Lord, to do according to all that is written in this book."

Huldah Prophesies Disaster

²² So Hilkiah and those whom the king had sent went to Huldah the prophetess, the wife of Shallum the son of Tokhath, son of Hasrah, keeper of the wardrobe (now she lived in Jerusalem in the Second Quarter) and spoke to her to that effect. ²³ And she said to them, "Thus says the Lord, the God of Israel: 'Tell the man who sent you to me, ²⁴ Thus says the Lord, Behold, I will bring disaster upon this place and upon its inhabitants, all the curses that are written in the book that was read before the king of Judah. ²⁵ Because they have forsaken me and have made offerings to other gods, that they might provoke me to anger with all the works of their hands, therefore my wrath will be poured out on this place and will not be quenched. ²⁶ But to the king of Judah, who sent you to inquire of the Lord, thus shall you say to him, Thus says the Lord, the God of Israel: Regarding the words that you have heard, ²⁷ because your heart was tender and you humbled yourself before God when you heard his words against this place and its inhabitants, and you have humbled yourself before me and have torn your clothes and wept before me, I also have heard you, declares the Lord. ²⁸ Behold, I will gather you to your fathers, and you shall be gathered to your grave in peace, and your eyes shall not see all the disaster that I will bring upon this place and its inhabitants.'" And they brought back word to the king.

²⁹ Then the king sent and gathered together all the elders of Judah and Jerusalem. ³⁰ And the king went up to the house of the LORD, with all the men of Judah and the inhabitants of Jerusalem and the priests and the Levites, all the people both great and small. And he read in their hearing all the words of the Book of the Covenant that had been found in the house of the LORD. ³¹ And the king stood in his place and made a covenant before the LORD, to walk after the LORD and to keep his commandments and his testimonies and his statutes, with all his heart and all his soul, to perform the words of the covenant that were written in this book. ³² Then he made all who were present in Jerusalem and in Benjamin join in it. And the inhabitants of Jerusalem did according to the covenant of God, the God of their fathers. ³³ And Josiah took away all the abominations from all the territory that belonged to the people of Israel and made all who were present in Israel serve the LORD their God. All his days they did not turn away from following the LORD, the God of their fathers.

Josiah Keeps the Passover

35 Josiah kept a Passover to the LORD in Jerusalem. And they slaughtered the Passover lamb on the fourteenth day of the first month. ² He appointed the priests to their offices and encouraged them in the service of the house of the LORD. ³ And he said to the Levites who taught all Israel and who were holy to the LORD, "Put the holy ark in the house that Solomon the son of David, king of Israel, built. You need not carry it on your shoulders. Now serve the LORD your God and his people Israel. ⁴ Prepare yourselves according to your fathers' houses by your divisions, as prescribed in the writing of David king of

Israel and the document of Solomon his son. ⁵And stand in the Holy Place according to the groupings of the fathers' houses of your brothers the lay people, and according to the division of the Levites by fathers' household. ⁶And slaughter the Passover lamb, and consecrate yourselves, and prepare for your brothers, to do according to the word of the LORD by Moses."

⁷ Then Josiah contributed to the lay people, as Passover offerings for all who were present, lambs and young goats from the flock to the number of 30,000, and 3,000 bulls; these were from the king's possessions. ⁸And his officials contributed willingly to the people, to the priests, and to the Levites. Hilkiah, Zechariah, and Jehiel, the chief officers of the house of God, gave to the priests for the Passover offerings 2,600 Passover lambs and 300 bulls. ⁹Conaniah also, and Shemaiah and Nethanel his brothers, and Hashabiah and Jeiel and Jozabad, the chiefs of the Levites, gave to the Levites for the Passover offerings 5,000 lambs and young goats and 500 bulls.

¹⁰When the service had been prepared for, the priests stood in their place, and the Levites in their divisions according to the king's command. ¹¹ And they slaughtered the Passover lamb, and the priests threw the blood that they received from them while the Levites flayed the sacrifices. ¹²And they set aside the burnt offerings that they might distribute them according to the groupings of the fathers' houses of the lay people, to offer to the LORD, as it is written in the Book of Moses. And so they did with the bulls. ¹³And they roasted the Passover lamb with fire according to the rule; and they boiled the holy offerings in pots, in cauldrons, and in pans, and carried them quickly to all the lay people. ¹⁴And afterward they prepared for themselves and for the priests, because the priests, the sons of Aaron, were

offering the burnt offerings and the fat parts until night; so the Levites prepared for themselves and for the priests, the sons of Aaron. ¹⁵ The singers, the sons of Asaph, were in their place according to the command of David, and Asaph, and Heman, and Jeduthun the king's seer; and the gatekeepers were at each gate. They did not need to depart from their service, for their brothers the Levites prepared for them.

¹⁶ So all the service of the LORD was prepared that day, to keep the Passover and to offer burnt offerings on the altar of the LORD, according to the command of King Josiah. ¹⁷ And the people of Israel who were present kept the Passover at that time, and the Feast of Unleavened Bread seven days. ¹⁸ No Passover like it had been kept in Israel since the days of Samuel the prophet. None of the kings of Israel had kept such a Passover as was kept by Josiah, and the priests and the Levites, and all Judah and Israel who were present, and the inhabitants of Jerusalem. ¹⁹ In the eighteenth year of the reign of Josiah this Passover was kept.

Josiah Killed in Battle

²⁰ After all this, when Josiah had prepared the temple, Neco king of Egypt went up to fight at Carchemish on the Euphrates, and Josiah went out to meet him. ²¹ But he sent envoys to him, saying, "What have we to do with each other, king of Judah? I am not coming against you this day, but against the house with which I am at war. And God has commanded me to hurry. Cease opposing God, who is with me, lest he destroy you." ²² Nevertheless, Josiah did not turn away from him, but disguised himself in order to fight with him. He did not listen to the words of Neco from the mouth of God, but came to fight in the plain

of Megiddo. ²³ And the archers shot King Josiah. And the king said to his servants, "Take me away, for I am badly wounded." ²⁴ So his servants took him out of the chariot and carried him in his second chariot and brought him to Jerusalem. And he died and was buried in the tombs of his fathers. All Judah and Jerusalem mourned for Josiah. ²⁵ Jeremiah also uttered a lament for Josiah; and all the singing men and singing women have spoken of Josiah in their laments to this day. They made these a rule in Israel; behold, they are written in the Laments. ²⁶ Now the rest of the acts of Josiah, and his good deeds according to what is written in the Law of the Lord, ²⁷ and his acts, first and last, behold, they are written in the Book of the Kings of Israel and Judah.

Judah's Decline

36 The people of the land took Jehoahaz the son of Josiah and made him king in his father's place in Jerusalem. ² Jehoahaz was twenty-three years old when he began to reign, and he reigned three months in Jerusalem. ³ Then the king of Egypt deposed him in Jerusalem and laid on the land a tribute of a hundred talents of silver and a talent of gold. ⁴ And the king of Egypt made Eliakim his brother king over Judah and Jerusalem, and changed his name to Jehoiakim. But Neco took Jehoahaz his brother and carried him to Egypt.

⁵ Jehoiakim was twenty-five years old when he began to reign, and he reigned eleven years in Jerusalem. He did what was evil in the sight of the Lord his God. ⁶ Against him came up Nebuchadnezzar king of Babylon and bound him in chains to take him to Babylon. ⁷ Nebuchadnezzar also carried part of the vessels of the house of the Lord to Babylon and put them in his palace in Babylon. ⁸ Now the rest of the acts of Jehoiakim,

and the abominations that he did, and what was found against him, behold, they are written in the Book of the Kings of Israel and Judah. And Jehoiachin his son reigned in his place.

⁹ Jehoiachin was eighteen years old when he became king, and he reigned three months and ten days in Jerusalem. He did what was evil in the sight of the LORD. ¹⁰ In the spring of the year King Nebuchadnezzar sent and brought him to Babylon, with the precious vessels of the house of the LORD, and made his brother Zedekiah king over Judah and Jerusalem.

¹¹ Zedekiah was twenty-one years old when he began to reign, and he reigned eleven years in Jerusalem. ¹² He did what was evil in the sight of the LORD his God. He did not humble himself before Jeremiah the prophet, who spoke from the mouth of the LORD. ¹³ He also rebelled against King Nebuchadnezzar, who had made him swear by God. He stiffened his neck and hardened his heart against turning to the LORD, the God of Israel. ¹⁴ All the officers of the priests and the people likewise were exceedingly unfaithful, following all the abominations of the nations. And they polluted the house of the LORD that he had made holy in Jerusalem.

¹⁵ The LORD, the God of their fathers, sent persistently to them by his messengers, because he had compassion on his people and on his dwelling place. ¹⁶ But they kept mocking the messengers of God, despising his words and scoffing at his prophets, until the wrath of the LORD rose against his people, until there was no remedy.

Jerusalem Captured and Burned

¹⁷ Therefore he brought up against them the king of the Chaldeans, who killed their young men with the sword in the

house of their sanctuary and had no compassion on young man or virgin, old man or aged. He gave them all into his hand. ¹⁸ And all the vessels of the house of God, great and small, and the treasures of the house of the LORD, and the treasures of the king and of his princes, all these he brought to Babylon. ¹⁹ And they burned the house of God and broke down the wall of Jerusalem and burned all its palaces with fire and destroyed all its precious vessels. ²⁰ He took into exile in Babylon those who had escaped from the sword, and they became servants to him and to his sons until the establishment of the kingdom of Persia, ²¹ to fulfill the word of the LORD by the mouth of Jeremiah, until the land had enjoyed its Sabbaths. All the days that it lay desolate it kept Sabbath, to fulfill seventy years.

The Proclamation of Cyrus

²² Now in the first year of Cyrus king of Persia, that the word of the LORD by the mouth of Jeremiah might be fulfilled, the LORD stirred up the spirit of Cyrus king of Persia, so that he made a proclamation throughout all his kingdom and also put it in writing: ²³ "Thus says Cyrus king of Persia, 'The LORD, the God of heaven, has given me all the kingdoms of the earth, and he has charged me to build him a house at Jerusalem, which is in Judah. Whoever is among you of all his people, may the LORD his God be with him. Let him go up.'"